WHEN

A LIFETIME OF

GOLF IS

FUN AND ADVENTURE

A BALL

IN THE GAME

Dr. Gary Wiren

CLOCK
TOWER
PRESS

For information address   Clock Tower Press
                          3622 W. Liberty Rd.
                          Ann Arbor, MI 48103

Cover design by Bruce Worden

All photos from the personal collection of the author except:
p. 61 Courtesy of The PGA of America
p. 112 Courtesy of the *Omaha World Herald*
p. 192 Courtesy of the Swedish Sport Federation

Library of Congress Cataloging-in-Publication Data:

Wiren, Gary.
When golf is a ball : a lifetime of fun and adventure in the game / Gary Wiren.
p. cm.
ISBN 1-932202-17-X
1. Golf—Anecdotes. I. Title.
GV967.W72 2004
796.352—dc22
2004016320

To all from whom I have learned...
teachers, friends, fellow professionals,
competitors, lovers of golf, and family.

CONTENTS

ACKNOWLEDGMENTS

I owe thanks to so many. My late father, Lynn, who let me, at nine years of age, carry his canvas bag and hit a few shots when he played at Spring Lake Park Municipal Golf Course in Omaha, Nebraska. To "Babe" Etter, the pro there who came to me when I was 12 and said, "Kid, I like the way you handle yourself. Would you like to work here?" To my golfing friends in high school and college, more than I have room to note, except for my best friend and college teammate, Dr. Richard Tschetter. Thanks to the young man I taught at the University of Michigan (his name has long escaped me). He told me that Meadowbrook Country Club (outside of Detroit) was looking for an assistant pro and asked if I would be interested. His father was on the selection committee. I got the job. That job at a first-rate private club was an eye-opener to the big time. The head professional there, Paul Shepard, made it an enjoyable and productive experience.

Gratitude would be an inadequate word to use to thank the Hope family at Oakway Golf Course in Eugene, Oregon for the opportunity to develop my skills that led to a specialty in teaching golf. That position as head professional also allowed me to form a working relationship with the local newspaper, *The Eugene Register-Guard*, and the wonderful Baker family who still owns it. Together we promoted the Register-Guard Golf Schools that I conducted, teaching 14,000 people in nine years. I am also in debt to Wendall Wood, the professional from Eugene Country Club, who has worked there for over 80 years, first as caddy, then caddy master, assistant pro, head professional, professional emeritus, and now occasional gardener. He was my friend and sponsor into the PGA. Appreciation to the Tommy Armour

Company with whom I enjoyed a 31-year relationship. "Domo Arrigato" (thank you) to my many Japanese friends including the former IGR staff and the wonderful Mizuno family. I had 20 years of courteous and kind treatment. I owe many thanks to my friends at the National Golf Foundation, who chose me to write for them, teach in seminars, and who have honored me with one of their highest awards, "The Graffis." I owe a great debt of gratitude to the many people, particularly my fellow PGA pros and my LPGA friends (several of whom are mentioned in this book), who have helped me to learn and grow in the game. Most certainly I owe a large thank you to the PGA of America. By employing me, they gave me the opportunity to take my thoughts and ideas about the game and teaching beyond the regional to the world stage. In so doing I was fortunate enough to be exposed to many of the game's great people.

Finally, to my wonderful wife, Ione, and my family—Trace, Paige, Bryn, and Dane—who were strong through times when I traveled, which was often, and supportive every moment. They all helped me with this book, as they have done in other projects in my life. I am proud of each one of them for the people they are and I love them all.

Twenty years in Japan, often on the stage.

Introduction

My wife, four children and I were living in Eugene, Oregon, home of the University of Oregon, with which I was affiliated. While there, I was invited to come to Palm Beach Gardens, Florida, to serve as the Education Director for the PGA of America. At that time my career path still offered other directions, particularly in the world of academia. So when the opportunity came to devote my daily activities and career toward golf, my wife questioned me. "Are we going to always be around people who just talk about what they hit on hole number 17 and how many putts they had that day, or is our life going to have more substance?" I assured her that we would be meeting and dealing with quality people, and that the choices in our lives of maintaining balance beyond golf would be ours. Fortunately, it has turned out just that way. Our friends are varied, our conversations interesting, and what someone hit on number 17 comes up only on occasion. While I enjoy a wide variety of activities, this book is about that portion of my life that revolves around golf.

Golf was fun when I started to play at 10 and has lost little since its first captivation. Golf has been fun as a competitor, writer, collector, speaker, administrator, and businessman, but mostly as a teacher. It has been fun to meet famous golfers like Walter Hagen, Sam Snead and Byron Nelson, Arnold Palmer, Gary Player, Jack Nicklaus, and many others. And to have people like Bill Gates, Warren Buffett, and Jack Welch come to my home because golf is special to them as well.

An adventure? Most certainly! My wife, Ione, and I have traveled to 32 countries with golf as the reason. Because of golf in my life I have had the opportunity to walk on the Great Wall of China, in the tulip gardens of Holland, up the Tobel in Switzerland, around the Coliseum in Italy, and within the Royal Grounds in Denmark; to enjoy a sauna in Finland, eat sauerkraut and dumplings in the Czech Republic; teach beauty pageant contestants in Curaçao; chase dingo dogs in the Australian outback; sing in Singapore; taste a Sacher torte in Austria; gamble at the casino in Monaco; fish the lakes of New Zealand; meet geishas in Japan; and sail the Mediterranean aboard the fabulous *Sea Cloud*. It certainly has been an adventure.

Those fun and adventurous parts of my life that have made golf "a ball" provide the experiences, stories, quotes, quips, and observations that make up the content of this book. It has been written with the intent of providing information, entertainment, and inspiration to those who savor its pages.

All that you read here is presented to the best of my memory. I apologize in advance if there are any omissions, embellishments, or incorrect facts as a result of the passing of time, but the essence is always there. If I have failed to acknowledge anyone from whom I may have received material or who has shared a story, I apologize.

A Personal Philosophy

When someone comes to me to begin the game of golf, I ask him or her several questions: Why do you want to learn the game? How much time do you have to spend in practice or play? What is your occupation? Do you have hobbies and, if so, what are they? Have you played other sports? Do you have any physical limitations? Are there friends or family who play that you can join?

Then I explain that when someone takes up a new activity it is wise to find out what it takes to succeed. In golf there are six elements that influence one's playing performance. They are:

1. Biomechanical Technique
2. Psychological Strength
3. Physical Fitness
4. Quality and Quantity of Practice
5. Game Knowledge (playing from unusual lies and weather conditions, rules, specialty shots, etc.)
6. Correct Equipment

That information will help us lay out a plan for learning the game.

For the game of life it is even more important to have a plan based upon what it takes to produce a meaningful time on Earth. I have created a personal philosophy that is a guide for that plan. A framed calligraphy copy hangs in our home's dining room. Here is what it says:

Philosophy of Life

*Continue to grow throughout your life by study
and by experience*

Care for the earth and your surroundings

*Have compassion for God's creatures and love for your
fellow man*

*Work hard and play hard in a positive and enthusiastic
way*

Train your body—it is the only one you will ever have

*Seek a relationship with the Almighty and see
your spirit as a special gift.*

Some Things You May Not Know About Famous Golfers

Golfers like to hear stories about their heroes, particularly when they contain something personal or humorous, or might have some small bit of instruction attached. Many such stories have been told, but I hope you will find these to be fresh and appealing.

IT TOOK A WHILE, BUT HE GOT IT BACK

On the way to a pro-am in South Florida, Bill Baber, one of our foursome, shared this story with me:

> I was the club champion at the Skokie Country Club in Chicago the year we celebrated the 30th anniversary of Gene Sarazen's 1922 U.S. Open Victory. It was a stellar event with an exhibition round that featured a foursome of: Jock Hutchison, who had been our pro at Skokie in 1922 and later won the British Open; Chick Evans, an earlier Open and Amateur champion of America who also played in the '22 event; Sarazen, the

1

eventual winner; and me. That evening we had a wonderful banquet with a full house. One after another, the star players came to the podium and reminisced, Sarazen being the featured speaker. Dressed in his plus

A happy Gene Sarazen holding The British Open trophy.

fours, jacket, and tie, he was the image of a dashing celebrity who was in especially good humor that night. His highlight story told of how the final competition on Sunday was played over 36 holes, the custom in earlier Opens. Sarazen had been paired with Jock, who had had an excellent morning 18 holes and was moving into contention. There was only a short interval between the rounds, during which Gene needed to take a restroom break. He located a men's room that was in a basement facility underneath the clubhouse. He described it as having an oiled dirt floor that slanted back up to a pair of enclosed stools. While Sarazen was at the urinal, a ball rolled down from the toilets behind, obviously having fallen out of the trousers of someone seated on one of the stools. That someone happened to be Jock. Gene picked it up and put it in his pocket, washed his hands, and headed for a quick bite and then the first tee. When he got to the tee there was no sign of Hutchison. When Jock finally arrived, he appeared flustered and out of sorts. Hutchison played poorly in the afternoon, falling out of contention.

At that point in the story, Sarazen turned from the microphone, reached in his pocket and pulled out an old ball with the mesh markings from the 1920s. Facing Jock he said, "Jock, I've had this ball all those years and I want to return it to you tonight because I think it will make you feel better." The house broke into laughter followed by a standing round of applause.

Bing Gets Zinged

Many of Bing Crosby's fans have known that the world's most popular crooner was a golfer, but did you know he was accomplished enough to have played in the British Amateur Championship? He loved golf and started the world's first pro-celebrity golf tournament that came to be known simply as "The Crosby." He also performed two songs about golf—"Straight Down the Middle," and "Tomorrow's My Lucky Day."

Bing was a member at the venerable Cypress Point Golf Club on the Monterey Peninsula. It is an extremely private establish-

Bing Crosby's singing voice was known around the world. His golf ability was also known at St. Andrews.

ment that knows only limited play. On some of winter's cool stormy days you are hard pressed to find more than a handful of people there playing golf. It was just such a blustery day when Bing and some friends were on the course. A member happened to come by the clubhouse and went upstairs to the top where there is a spot from which one can look out unto the course. Using the available binoculars, he scanned the links and found Bing's group on the famous 16th hole, one of the toughest par-3s in the world. What he saw next astounded him. Bing stepped to the tee and with a wood club knocked his shot onto the green and into the cup for a hole-in-one, a seemingly impossible feat on that hole, especially given the weather!

It was a known fact that Bing was generous with his time but a bit tight with his pennies. When a player performs the feat of acing a hole as he had just done, it is customary to buy a round of drinks for all who are present. But for whom was he going to buy? There was no one in the clubhouse. Our member was inspired. Sensing an opportunity, he immediately got on the phone and started calling people, telling them what happened and asking them to call others then get right down to the club. By the time Bing's group finished the 16th, then the 17th, and the 18th, the crowd was starting to arrive. They kept coming until the nearly empty parking lot overflowed. And that is how Bing got Zinged.

THE DEMISE OF THE MOLE CRICKETS

Let me tell you about Jerry Tucker, but also let me warn you, you may not believe it. Jerry may be the most compulsive record keeper in PGA history. He can tell you how many pages he has completed in each of the current four books he is reading; how many words his dog understands; what his seasonal bowling average was in, say 1987, along with each score and more; but his golf stats are the best. Ask him what he shot on a given day 15 years ago and he will offer you not only the scores and the names of the people he played with, but also greens in regulation, putts, temperature, wind, ball type and number, what he had for breakfast, his attitude rating for the day, and even if he had sex the night before he played. These stats are all compiled in notebooks, allowing him to make comparisons with previous years. Now you would think his behavior is odd, or even that he might be a bit of a nerd, but he is far from it. He is an excellent competitive golfer, having had his moments on the PGA and Senior PGA Tours (now Champions Tour). He is talented in pocket billiards, ping-pong, darts, and any other skill contests you can think of, plus being the king of trivia.

Jerry's last position as a head professional was at that great St. Louis club, Bellerive, site of the 1965 U.S. Open and the 1992 PGA Championship. According to Jerry, a couple of weeks before the 1992 PGA, this is what happened:

> One of my assistants said that Arnold Palmer was on the phone wanting to talk to me. Although I tried to be cool in front of my staff, I was pretty excited as Arnie was my idol. I picked up the phone and Arnie said, "Jerry, I wonder if you could play a practice round with me before the tournament?" I told him that I felt I could work it into my schedule, so we made the arrangement. When the day arrived I asked my dad, who had come in to help the staff in setting up the merchandise tents, to walk around with us. Arnie was wonderful to my dad. In fact when we were going down the second fairway and Arnie was walking with my father, it was one of the few times in my life that I had a tear come to my eye.
>
> Arnie was excited as he made birdies on 9, 10, and 11; he even got his old pants-hitching routine going. He lived up to every expectation I ever had. His caddy,

Royce, told me about Arnie making himself available for 45 minutes before or after a round to sign autographs. His eye was actually injured the week before at the Ameritech tournament when someone had shoved a pen at him trying to get an autograph and accidentally poked him right in the eye.

A humorous part of the day started on the 15th green. Although I didn't hear anything, Arnie had a "breaking wind" episode. When he did, he apparently looked at Royce, winked, smiled, and said, "Royce, did you hear that mole cricket?"

I overheard the comment and innocently responded, "I know they have them in Florida, Arnie, but I don't think we have any mole crickets here in St. Louis."

Royce looked at me and said, "Jerry, I think Arnie made that noise."

So when Arnie did it again on the next green, then looked at Royce and winked saying, "I think I heard another mole cricket," I now understood what was going on.

I told him, "Okay, okay, I've got it now."

The round was over too soon, but afterward Arnie posed for pictures with my parents. I sent Arnie the pictures to sign, which he did and sent them back. He was very gracious. So I sent him a thank you note for asking me to play and being so nice to my family. I wrote on the card: "Arnie, It was a wonderful experience to play with you and see you make those birdies. I wish you could save them for the tournament. Thanks again. I hope we can play some time in the future. P.S. After you left, I had our green superintendent spray for those mole crickets, but we haven't seen or heard any since you were here."

PINPOINT ACCURACY

In earlier days at the Masters, players would use the local caddies from the club. The practice of hiring a regular year-round full-time caddy for all events was unheard of. The caddies at Augusta wore the white uniforms with the player's name on the back, a practice that has since been copied by many tournaments. At the practice range the caddy would dump his player's shag bag of balls out at the player's feet, and then take his spot in the practice area to chase the balls. If you were caddying for a really good player, there wasn't much chasing. The player would start out with a few sand wedge shots pitched to the caddy's feet, and then gradually move the caddy back as he progressed through the clubs. It was sometimes dangerous when the hitting stations were full and the range chock-a-block with white uniformed men holding small bags, dodging balls coming from all directions. Former Master's Champion Jimmy Demaret, the fun-loving story-telling king of the Tour, had finished his practice session and retired to the locker room. One of the players asked him as he walked by, "Jimmy, how's Hogan hitting it?"

"Not bad," said Demaret. "When I left he was working on his one-iron, hit his caddy on the head, and then hit him twice more on the way down."

Jimmy could entertain.

Ben Hogan at Carnoustie—1953.

No Matter What It Takes!

Jay Hebert, former PGA Champion and one of the most likeable professionals on the Tour, came to the PGA Junior Golf Academy as the "Tour Player of the Week." He demonstrated to the campers not only a beautiful swing, but also the personality and manner of a southern gentleman from Louisiana. Jay was a handsome man with a winning way. When he said something in his strong deep voice he said it with conviction. Jay was really respected and well liked by the kids. While hitting wedge shots during his demonstration on the range, he stopped, held up his wedge, and said, "This is one of the most important clubs in the bag. I'm telling you right now to get yourself a good wedge. *I don't care how you get it, just get a good wedge!*"

That was on a Tuesday. On Thursday we had skit night where the campers, with the help of their counselor-coach, put on a short play poking fun at the camp and the staff. It was always an entertaining evening as you got to see yourself portrayed in a humorous light. One of the teams came onto the stage with their entire group, minus one, mimicking hitting balls on the range. Some campers pretended to be staff pros helping others, but doing it in a way that would draw laughs. Others made goofy swings that supposedly they had learned that day. Then from out of the wings the missing camper came running in, very excited and holding a club up over his head, yelling, "I got it, I got it!"

"What did you get?" the rest asked in unison.

"I got me a wedge."

"Where did you get it?" the group came back.

"*I stole it out of Jay Hebert's bag!*"

It was the biggest laugh of the week.

You're a What?

One of Gary Player's favorite stories that he tells on himself is when he recalls the first time he played in the Open Championship, that year held on the Old Course at St. Andrews. A complete unknown out of South Africa, Player was announced on the tee and proceeded to hit, on the widest fairway in golf, a wild hook almost out-of-bounds near the road on the 18th hole. When he came back from his shot and was waiting for the next contestants to hit, the starter asked him what his handicap was. "I don't have a handicap sir, I'm a professional," said Player.

The starter looked at him incredulously and said, *"You must be a damned good chipper and putter."*

The Greatest Record in the Books

If you were to rate the greatest feat in golf, there would be several contenders. Maybe Jack Nicklaus' driving the 18th hole in The Open at St. Andrews four days in succession; possibly Joe Ezar's call shot 64 in Europe when he said he would shoot 64, wrote the scores for each hole down before he played, missed the predicted score on only two, and shot the 64, breaking the course record; or consider Clarence Doser, PGA club pro from the Mid-Atlantic Section, shooting his age 1,644 times; then there is Freddie McLeod's ringer score of 39 for 18 holes at Columbia Country Club in Chevy Chase, Maryland, made over a period that covered the 59 years he served there. These are all amazing feats. But the one I rate right up there is revealed in this story.

Rick Acton ended his golf career way too early, losing to cancer at the age of 53 while still serving at Sahalee Golf Club in

Blaine, Washington. His playing record would easily put him in with the greatest golfers ever to come out of the Pacific Northwest, having had success on both the PGA Tour and PGA Senior Tour as well as winning every major regional title in his part of the country. While still learning the ropes as a young tour player he stopped in to play a round of golf at the public Papago Park in Phoenix, Arizona. Rick was a great putter but happened to be a switch hitter. By that I mean that he played right-handed but putted left-handed. There have been a few other good players who used that method. After finishing the front nine at Papago and shooting a 32 he got interested enough to go into the pro shop to ask the veteran professional, Arch Watkins, the following question: "What's the course record out there?"

In a kind of crusty reply, Arch said, "Right-handed or left-handed?"

Now that was an interesting response considering Acton's playing style, but Rick answered, "Right-handed."

"Sixty-three, Johnny Bulla."

After a pause, Acton asked, "What is it left-handed?"

Again Arch answered, but this time it was, "Sixty-two, Johnny Bulla."

And that would be my entry into a greatest-golf-feats-of-all-time contest.

THE MASTER KEY FOR JONES

At Eastlake Golf Club in Atlanta where Bobby Jones grew up, the transplanted Scot, Stewart Maiden, was his teacher. Not only was Maiden his teacher, but also he was his swing model. It was said that from a distance it was often hard to tell whether it was Jones or Maiden swinging the club.

In 1925 Jones was headed for the Worcester Country Club in

Massachusetts to play in the U.S. Open. The first two practice rounds were a disaster for Jones. He shot two medal scores in the 80s. After the second disastrous struggle on the links he immediately called back to Eastlake and asked Maiden to catch the next train to Worcester to see if Stewart could put his swing straight. Maiden rode all night and arrived at the club the next morning, the day before the start of the tournament. They took a couple of sacks of balls out to the practice area. Jones went through the first sack without a word of coaching from Maiden, who was known as a man of few words. Halfway through the next sack Maiden gave his only comment, then turned and left. The comment was, *"Why don't you try hitting it on your back swing!"* End of lesson.

While given succinctly, the message was accurate. Jones' success as a player leaned heavily on his rhythm and timing. Maiden recognized that Jones was rushing his back swing and the facetious remark might get him to sense that. By slowing the back swing, Jones would recapture his rhythm and his glorious swing. He must have, because he tied for

Jones' swing looks impeccable here.

the U.S. Open Championship that year, losing by a stroke in a playoff. He posted no scores in the 80s because his mentor could identify the one single key that would make all the rest of the moves fall into line.

WHO REALLY CARES?

Orville Moody was one of the surprise champions of the U.S. Open, having won in 1967, his only victory as a PGA Tour player. But beyond that, for an Open Champion, his record was not impressive. Though he is a likeable guy and a talented player, his career as a star was short-lived. Putting proved to be his nemesis, getting so bad that his scores

Miller Barber called it as he saw it.

even caused him to fail to garner many sponsor's tournament exemptions. During this period when he did manage an exemption, he apparently did not fare well in the event. He stormed into the players' locker and food area and announced to the gathering that he had *nine* on a hole. "I had a nine out there today, a nine! How can a guy who's won the U.S. Open have a nine, and with no penalty strokes? I hit it nine times!" The room was quiet, but Orville started in again. "A nine, nine shots on one hole!"

It was about this time that Miller Barber, who had been only a listener up to now, became a speaker. "Orville, let me tell you something. Half the guys in this room are happy as hell you had a nine. *The other half wish you'd a had a ten!"*

Note: Moody's ball striking skills were affirmed when he joined the Champion's Tour and garnered 11 victories, aided by the use of the long putter.

A LESSON FROM "THE HAIG"

Melvin "Chick" Harbert is a Member of the PGA Golf Hall of Fame, having won The PGA Championship, 10 Tour events, and over 50 long-drive titles when such events were held weekly as

an attraction prior to the tournament. A reporter who was not a fan of the affable and self-assured Chick once asked him before the Masters, "Harbert, what is your objective in golf?"

In keeping with Chick's nature, he replied, "To eliminate the second shot."

Harbert earned the nickname Chick when he was a tyke about

Harbert became a big hitter.

five years old. His father was a golf professional who had invited the great Open and Amateur Champion Chick Evans (founder of the Evans Caddy Scholarship program) to give an exhibition at the senior Harbert's course. Little Melvin followed Evans around during his practice round and throughout the match. For the next several days he tried to mimic Evans' swing. People started calling Melvin "Little Chick" because of his obvious exhibitionism. Later they just dropped the "Little."

One of the more memorable events that happened to the young Harbert was a visit from Walter Hagen. "Pop" Harbert again had arranged an exhibition, but this time the great Hagen was the performer. When the now-teenaged Chick asked his dad who Hagen was going to play in the match, his dad replied, "You." Chick protested and pleaded that he didn't want to have to play the famous Hagen, but his father did not relent.

When the day so feared by Chick arrived, he was up early and out practicing hours before the 1 p.m. match. As the clock moved closer to the starting time, Chick's hands were sweaty and well exercised, but no Hagen was in sight. With close to 1,000 spectators gathered for the event, it was another 10 minutes before a chauffeur-driven sedan pulled into the parking lot, scattering gravel as it came to a halt. Out stepped the princely Hagen, dressed to the nines. "Sorry folks, a bit of a delay getting here, but let me hit a few warm-ups and we are off," said the broadly smiling Hagen.

As Harbert told it, the introductions were made on the first tee, with a goodly amount of attention paid to "The Haig's" playing record. Up to this point Harbert had no record to speak of, but in a couple of years, as an amateur, he would lead the Michigan Open by 17 shots after three rounds. The players were off, with Hagen chatting up the crowd, hitting good shots, and going on his merry way while paying absolutely no attention to Harbert, his opponent. This continued for four holes with Chick wondering if he was the invisible man. On the fifth tee, Hagen put his arm around Chick and said, "How you feeling, kid? You looked a little peaked on the first few holes."

Well that got Harbert mad. He said to himself, *I'm going to beat this old so-and-so.* Then Chick's confidence and game began to improve. By the 18th, Harbert was only one shot back. He had knocked his approach on the green about 15 feet from the hole, with Hagen about eight feet from the cup. If he made it and Hagen missed, Harbert would tie the living legend. So as Chick himself described it, "I plumb-bobbed my putt. Then I got down on all fours to better read the line from behind the ball. I went to the other side of the hole and repeated the plumb-bob and the four point reading-the-green position. Back at my ball, I took a long time before stroking it and managed to roll it right into the cup."

"The Haig." Never another quite like him.

Hagen looked at Harbert, who now revealed a "Take that, old man" look on his face. Then the great Haig, always the showman, proceeded to mimic Harbert's every previous action. He plumb-bobbed from behind the ball, and then got on all fours on both sides of the hole just as Harbert had done. He finally approached the ball, turned his putter blade around to the back side, and standing from the left-hand position, easily stroked the ball in for the win. He came over to Harbert and said, "Nice match kid."

"I felt about six inches tall," said Chick, "but that was The Haig."

MILLER IN THE WOODS

I really like Johnny Miller as a golf commentator. He's honest, yet fair. John has come up with some memorable funny lines both in the broadcast booth and out of it. As a player he always had a strong belief in the value of using visualization during a competitive round. Early in his career he once said he had three images to help his swing. If he wanted to hit a fade he pictured Lee Trevino. If he wanted produce a draw he would visualize Tony Lema. And if the picture was to be a straight shot he envisioned his own swing. John would just choose to picture the one that was working. It was particularly effective in his mind as he noted that it was very rare to have all three playing badly on the same day.

Johnny also used "WOOD cues." Cues are swing reminders, such as "Slow back," or "Swing through." The reason he called them WOOD cues was because that stands for *"Works Only One Day."*

JACK WHO?

It was 2002, the final year of the PGA Senior Championship at PGA National Golf Club. Unfortunately, it was also one of the wettest. Rain delays plagued the event, and the players were being shuttled back and forth from the course to the clubhouse more frequently than the players, officials, and certainly the gallery wanted. During one time-out, Jack Nicklaus, a previous winner of the event, was in the hallway thinking about getting a bite to eat. Large glass windows bordered the perimeter of the hallway and the function rooms where the players' lunch was being served. While Jack was making his decision, a male spectator of AARP age wearing glasses and a fisherman's hat tapped on the window to get Jack's attention, motioning for him to come over to open the glass double doors only a few feet away that led outside. Jack turned away, not in the mood to give an autograph

The Golden Bear gets a surprise.

at that moment, but the man persisted, tapping the window and signaling more vigorously for him to come to the door. So, being the good sport, Jack went to the doors and pushed them open enough for the guy to stick his head inside. But instead of the expected autograph request, this fan said to Jack, "Have you seen Arnold Palmer in there?" The Golden Bear was…amused, and Arnold was even more so when he heard about it later.

A SPEEDY SQUIRE

Gene Sarazen was always noted for his fast play. No long pre-shot routines. Just select the club, step up, hit it, and get going. Jackson Bradley, a fine player out of Texas, once told me of meeting Sarazen as an opponent early in The PGA Championship, a match play event at the time. The match was over sooner than Jackson would have liked, with Sarazen the winner. Sitting in the locker room Bradley overheard Gene talking to the press in the next aisle saying, *"Well, I guess we ran that kid's legs off."*

A KNOCKOUT PUNCH

Golf professionals who can play both right-handed and left-handed are rare, but Bob Foppe, who served Kenwood Country Club in Cincinnati for many years, fits the description. Bob was a huge promoter of golf events, one of which was the "Boys Hope," that drew several high-level celebrities.

As Bob tells it:

> I happened to be paired with Bob Hope and Orville Moody. When we were playing, Mr. Hope said to me, "Bob, when we get to the fourth green I want you to

give me some advice around the green on how to hit the shot and then I'll try to do it. It won't come out the way I wanted and I'll appear irritated and take a swing at you with my fist. You just lean back and Orville will slap his hands and it will look and sound like I hit you in the jaw."

So I said, "Okay, just give me the word."

We reached the fourth tee and Hope said, "I'll try to play it down the right side to get into position."

I said, "With a big crowd like this I'm a little nervous. I don't know where I'll hit it."

As we got close to the green and Hope was ready to hit his little pitch shot, I went off to the side and announced to the gallery of several hundred people what kind of shot Hope should play and how he should do it. He hit the ball onto the green but it wasn't a very good shot, certainly not what he would have wanted. As we walked up to the green, Orville said, "Now!"

Hope turned to me and said, "Why, you gave me the wrong direction!" With that he swung. Unfortunately, I forgot to lean back and instead leaned forward. He hit me a good one. You may not be aware that early in his life, Bob Hope had been a pretty good amateur boxer. It took about five to six minutes before I woke up. It was the first knockout punch Bob Hope had thrown in his life...*ever*. I got an award from Perry Como for being the only guy who was dumb enough to walk into Hope instead away from him.

Getting a Little Help from "The King"

Bob Foppe tells of another exhibition they held at Kenwood with Hope, Perry Como, and Arnold Palmer.

> I had just put in a new practice range and decided to have yellow range balls. Now at the time, no one had ever heard of yellow range balls, so the first reaction from some of my members was not favorable. I had purchased the balls from Arnold Palmer's golf company, First Flight. Just before we were to start I cornered Palmer on the side and said, "Arnold, would you do me a favor?"
>
> "What is it, Bob?"
>
> "I need you to hit these yellow range balls."
>
> He looked at them and said, "Yellow range balls?"
>
> "Before you comment, Arnold, these are balls I bought from your company."
>
> He replied, "Bob, they are the finest range balls I've ever seen."
>
> "Would you go out on the tee and hit them with Mr. Hope and Mr. Como? The others will be there to hit them as well."
>
> So after Arnie hit some of these balls in front of several thousand people, he turned to the audience and said, "These are the finest range balls I've ever hit in my life. Where did you get them, Bob?"
>
> I said, "You know, I'm not sure if I remember what the company was, but I believe it was First Flight."
>
> He repeated, "Well, these are undoubtedly the finest range balls that I have ever hit." Then Como and Hope chimed in with similar support.

The next day some of the members who were complaining about the yellow golf balls arrived at the club. My comment to them was simply, "If they are good enough for Arnie, they should be good enough for you." There were no further complaints about yellow balls on the range.

Arnold helps the Kenwood pro.

The Goose and His Horde

J.C. Goosie was a former PGA Tour professional who probably gave more young players a start getting ready for the PGA Tour than anybody or any group. No, that's wrong. There is no *probably* in it. He DID give more players a start in their careers than anybody else. "Goose" organized the biggest, busiest successful mini-tour ever, which ran in Florida for 17 years. The list of players who cut their teeth on J.C.'s Florida Tour fills a lot of pages in the PGA Media Guide. But for every great success there were many more who didn't make it. Add them all up and we're talking big numbers and some real dollars.

His "graduates" used to kid him by saying, "Goose, you must be like Sam Snead and have millions stashed away buried in tin cans in your backyard."

J.C. would defuse their good-natured thrusts with, "Hell, you guys don't know what you're talking about." Then he would add, "But just for your own information, you can get $10,000 in hundreds into a #2 size can if you roll them real tight."

YOU Ain't No Sam Snead

The Boca Raton Hotel in Florida and professional Tommy Armour were synonymous during the 1950s and '60s. This is one of my favorite Armour stories. A member came into the pro shop looking for Tommy who happened to be there. The member told Armour that he had recently sold his business for a lot of money and was now retired. Explaining that he was still only 48 years old and was in good health, he wanted Tommy to teach him how to swing like Sam Snead. The man added that he didn't care what it cost and that he would give time to it, but that was his quest. Armour took a ball from the jar on the counter and escorted the member out of the pro shop to the putting green just outside. They walked to one of the cups on the green and Tommy took out the hole marker and rolled the ball into the cup.

"Now what I want you to do," he said, "is to reach down and pick up the ball from the cup." The man started to bend over while flex-

Tommy Armour was part psychologist, part teacher.

ing his knees to get down low enough to pick the ball up. Armour stopped him. "No, not like that. Reach down keeping your legs straight and pick it up."

The man made a feeble attempt but could only reach a few inches past his knees. Straining he said, "I can't do that."

"Well Snead can, so let's just teach you what *you* can do and forget about being Sam Snead."

I Think I've Got It

Because he served so long as a club professional at the fabled Oakland Hills Country Club in Detroit, few people remember how good a player Al Watrous was. He came within a whisker of winning the British Open; played on the very first Ryder Cup team, winning two points; and had 34 career victories, including the Canadian Open and Western Open. He was known as one of the first great golf "practicers." Does setting up a mat in the pro shop in the middle of a Michigan winter and hitting balls out into the snow through the open French doors give you the picture? That was Al.

I was doing some research for the PGA on the early Ryder Cup events and was trying to determine when in our fairly recent golfing history the players switched over from wooden to steel shafts. Since Al was involved right in the middle of that period I called from Palm Beach Gardens to his house in Dunedin, Florida, the PGA's former home, to seek some information. His daughter answered and said Al had gone back to Birmingham (a Detroit suburb) for the summer. Well it wasn't quite summer. In fact, it was still April and the weather wasn't that good in Michigan yet.

My next call was to his home up there. His wife answered and said, "Al is over at Don Soper's Driving Range in Royal Oak, practicing." That was interesting, because Al was 81 years old and I couldn't imagine what he might be practicing for.

My next call was to the range. When they answered the lady said, "Al is out hitting balls but if you want me to get him I will. Who is calling?" I gave her my name and waited.

Soon I heard a strong, friendly voice say, "Gary, how are you doing?"

"Great," I replied, "But what are you doing up there in April hitting balls in the cold?"

His response reflected the mind-set of millions of golfers and showed that the desire for improvement doesn't disappear with age. He said, "You know, *I'm working on something in my swing, and I think I've figured it out.*"

Note: A few years ago I received a call from a local man wanting a lesson. He said he was 63 years old and has been carrying a two handicap, which is pretty darn good golf. When I asked his name he said, "Tom Watrous."

"Are you any relation to Al Watrous?" I asked.

"He was my father," was the response. We set up a time, met, and when the lesson was over Tom said to me, "Gary, that is the first lesson I have ever taken, other than what my dad helped me with."

"Well Tom," I said, "That's ironic, because the first formal lesson I ever took was from your father."

Seeing Too Late

A contemporary of Al Watrous, also from Detroit, was Frank Walsh, professional for many years at Red Run Golf Club. He once finished as the runner-up in The PGA Championship when the tournament was at match play. Frank was not only a player, but also a keen student of the swing and a respected teacher. He was a friendly, affable man, who nonetheless was intense when it came to conversation about golf fundamentals and theories.

I was working on an historical black-and-white silent film from the archives of the PGA of America, trying to identify some of the players from the 1930s and '40s with whom I was unfamiliar. Seeking help, I called Frank, who enthusiastically agreed to meet me at the PGA office to assist. Frank appeared dressed in a smart-looking jacket, a silk handkerchief around his neck, a handful of flowers for the secretaries, and a smile on his face under his flowing white hair.

We went together to the conference room where I had set up

the film projector on a card table. Frank was having a great time as he watched the swings of some of his former adversaries. "There is 'Lighthorse' Harry Cooper, and that's Bill Mehlhorn, and good old 'Dutch' Harrison," he related as I wrote them down. Paul Runyan, Tommy Armour, Gene Sarazen, and several others were easy for me, but then Frank would come up with the ones I couldn't immediately identify, like Al Espinosa, Ky Lafoon, and Bobby Cruickshank.

But suddenly it was quiet. Then came this loud bang on the table that made the projector jump in the air. Frank had stood up, hit the table, and was angrily pacing. "Frank, what's the matter?" I asked.

He didn't say anything at first, and then he hit the table again while shouting, "Why couldn't I have seen that when I was playing?" Obviously Frank had picked up a swing thought while watching this film, one that had previously eluded him. The pain of not winning the "big one," The PGA in 1932, when he was in the finals, was still burning more than 40 years later.

No Presidential Pardon

For certain, the flamboyance of "the general," Arnold Palmer, helped fuel the golf boom of the 1960s and '70s. But the person who first ignited it was a real general (and later President), Dwight D. Eisenhower. "Ike" absolutely loved the game, playing it whenever and wherever he could. His addiction to and affection for the game most certainly was viewed by the public as a personal endorsement for golf. This, in turn, created a great deal of interest in getting others to try the game. While there was some political backlash to Eisenhower's frequent forays to the links, it didn't seem to diminish Ike's desire to play. Not even when the following bumper sticker appeared during his run for a second term: "BEN HOGAN FOR PRESIDENT… IF WE ARE GOING TO HAVE A GOLFER IN THE WHITE HOUSE, LET'S HAVE A GOOD ONE!"

Ike was considered to be just an average golfer with a handicap around 18, but he was a fierce competitor who loved to bet and hated to lose. In the midst of a close match at his favorite club, Burning Tree, and with a couple of bucks on the line, he found his drive at the 18th hole sitting awkwardly in the rough. He wasn't happy. Requesting the four-wood from his caddy, he proceeded to get a better angle for his swing by tamping the grass down behind the ball. The result was quite unexpected. The ball dropped deeper into the rough, making the shot almost impossible. "What in hell is going on here?" Ike shouted to his caddy.

Without hesitation he got the reply, "Well Mr. President, I figure you just over-improved your lie."

It Was a Present for Him, Not for Her

President Eisenhower loved his golf so much that he even used the White House grounds as a practice range. He also had a putting green built on the premises (if you want confirmation, check out the spike marks in the wood floor of the Oval Office). During his White House stay, he and his wife Mamie, seeking a quiet place to "get away from it all," bought a farm in Gettysburg, Pennsylvania. The farm, however, was devoid of any golf.

Ike, a member at Augusta National Country Club, was visiting The Masters tournament when he got into a conversation with Harry Moffitt, then president of the PGA of America. Moffitt inquired about the President's golfing opportunities at Gettysburg and wondered if he would like to have a putting green on which he could practice. Ike was delighted with the prospect, so Harry said he would take care of it.

Soon thereafter, Henry Poe received a call from Moffitt. Poe, later to be PGA president and at the time serving the Country Club in Reading, Pennsylvania, was informed that President Eisenhower had been promised a putting green. Although there were no funds set aside for the project, maybe Poe could "see what he could do." Poe got on the phone to several clubs in the area that might be willing to be of service to the President. He received confirmations from a few, who indicated that their golf superintendents could assist in getting the job done. So a meeting was scheduled with Poe and the President to discuss the location of the "green-to-be." Ike decided that he wanted it to be situated near the front porch so Mamie could sit there and watch him while he was practicing. In a few weeks, with the help from several nearby superintendents, a large 10,000-square-foot surface was shaped for putting, along with the installation of the proper drainage and irrigation. But, there was no grass.

It was time for another phone conversation between Moffitt and Poe. "How are things coming Henry?" asked Moffitt.

"Great," said Poe. "We have the green ready to go but we don't have any grass."

"Well," said Moffitt, "We don't have a budget for it, but see what you can do."

As though an angel were listening, Poe got a call the next day. It was Mr. W. R. Grace, the millionaire owner of the company by the same name. "I hear that you are building a putting green for the President down there at Gettysburg," said Grace, calling from Saucon Valley C.C. to the north in Bethlehem, Pennsylvania. "What are you doing for grass?"

"Well, we don't have any yet," responded Poe.

Grace continued, "We've got one of the best turf farms in the world here at Saucon. How much do you need?"

"Ten thousand square feet," Poe said hopefully.

"I'll have it sent down in few days along with a staff to install it," said Grace, and added, "They are artists."

True to his word, Grace had his staff there to finish off the prepared surface that became a putting green within hours. As Poe described it, "You could have putted on it that very day."

More than 30 years later Henry Poe went back to Gettysburg and visited the Eisenhower farm. Curious to see the result of his efforts years earlier, he walked out to the side of the house where the Presidential putting green had become a reality, but all that was there was the mounding where a green had once existed. Henry went over to a nearby

Ike loved his golf, wherever he was.

tree where years earlier a plaque had been attached. To Poe's surprise it was still there. Though now rusted, he could still read: "THIS GREEN WAS GIVEN TO PRESIDENT DWIGHT D. EISENHOWER AS A GIFT FROM THE PGA OF AMERICA." Noting Poe's interest in the plaque, a park ranger came over to ask if he could be of assistance. When Poe inquired about the demise of the green, the ranger said he had been here when they were still maintaining it. But one day, after the President had been deceased for several months, Mamie came out of the house when they were about to mow it and said, "Let that thing just be. I don't care if I ever see it again!"…Apparently, watching Ike putt was less enjoyable for her than it was for him.

SELECTIVE MEMORY

During the 1970s Jack Nicklaus used to spend a fair amount of time at the Frenchmen's Creek Golf Club in Palm Beach Gardens, Florida, a 36-hole layout that was the design of the late PGA Tour multiple winner Gardner Dickinson. It was Gardner's only effort, and it was a good one. The reason Jack hung out there was because Jack Grout, his teacher from Scioto C.C. in Columbus, Ohio, where Jack grew up, used Frenchmen's as a winter teaching spot. With Jack Grout there, along with Dickinson, noted club maker and teacher Toney Penna, and Nicklaus taking lessons, it was a "range rat's" dream...a continual daily golfing education.

One sunny Florida winter day Nicklaus was giving a corporate clinic, hitting shots and describing how he did it. It was typical Jack, one good shot after another, very Teutonic in its efficiency. Nearing his conclusion he asked the audience if there were any questions. "Yes, I have a question," offered a man in the first row. "How do you cure a shank?"

Jack smiled and replied, "I don't know. I never hit one." Jack turned away to field the next question from the other direction in the front row.

But before the question could be asked, the previous inquisitor boldly retorted. "I saw you hit one: U.S. Open, Pebble Beach, 14th hole!"

The smile left Jack's face. He slowly turned to face his accuser and stared at him with two blue lasers for what seemed like 30 seconds and then curtly replied, "I DON'T REMEMBER! NEXT QUESTION!" (This is a great example of how a champion player thinks. They have a selective memory, focusing on the positive; dismissing the negative.)

Do You Think You Can, or Think You Can't

This story involves Jack Nicklaus as well, but in a rather indirect way. The late Bert Yancey and I were rooming together while attending a golf outing at Peggy and Bullet Bell's Pine Needles Lodge in Southern Pines, North Carolina. Bert was one of the PGA Tour's premier players, having won seven events, including a runner-up U.S. Open finish. His ultimate golf dream, however, was to win The Masters. That vision was so powerful that he made clay models of each green at Augusta National and kept them under his bed when he wasn't studying the greens' unique contours.

Bert and I were talking late one night about the game and his career. He revealed this story. "You know, Gary, I have played 396 rounds of golf in tournaments where Jack Nicklaus was also competing. On those occasions I beat him 108 times. We were paired together 37 times.* When that was the case, I never beat him once.

Bert Yancey needed to believe he could.

I always felt that the gallery came out to watch Jack and I was just in the way." Though a fine player, Bert never did win The Masters, sadly enough. So it seems that Henry Ford was right when he said, "If you think you can, or you think you can't...you're right."

* The numbers are approximations from our conversation. I cannot recall the exact figures.

ONLY IN BOSTON

There are some stories that can take place only in certain localities. This is one of them…the place is Boston. Raymond Floyd was in his early years on the Tour when he found himself standing in a line leading to the ticket counter at Logan Airport in Boston. It was Sunday afternoon. That meant he had been an early starter off the tee on the final day of the Jimmy Fund Tournament. He was in line to change a ticket and check his luggage, moving it in incremental stages as each person ahead of him was waited on.

A very small and elderly lady in hat and gloves was walking in the concourse. As she approached Raymond, she noted his luggage included a large golf bag, the type that would be indicative of a professional player. She shuffled over to Raymond, tugged his coat jacket sleeve, looked up at him and said, "You a golfer, sonny?"

"Yes ma'am," replied Ray looking down and smiling.

"You play the Tour?" she continued.

"Yes ma'am, I do," he responded.

"You know Francis Ouimet?" she asked.

"No ma'am," said Ray with a bigger grin, "He was a little before my time." ***Only in Boston!***

Note: For the uninitiated, Francis Ouimet won the U.S. Open…in 1913!

HE JUST DIDN'T KNOW

Jack Whitaker, the TV sports personality with the mellifluous tones and great stories that make golf tournaments more interesting than simply revealing the scores, was doing a piece for TV with Ken Venturi in New York. After the shoot was over Whitaker asked Venturi, the former U.S. Open Champ, if he wanted to play golf the next day. Ken said that he didn't have his clubs, shoes, or golf clothes, but inquired as to what Jack had in mind. Winged Foot, where Whitaker is a member, was the answer. That raised the interest level for Ken, because Winged Foot is always a treat. Venturi was told by Whitaker that he had extra golf clothes in his locker that would work since they were both about the same size, the locker attendant could get him some shoes, and Jack had an extra set of old clubs that Ken could use. So the match was set.

The next morning, accompanied by a caddy, they were off on the fabled course. Venturi was playing in borrowed shoes, a floppy fisherman's style cap, outdated golf shirt, wrinkled slacks, and a set of clubs that had yet to hear of high tech. Nonetheless, Ken was on his game. Two under through eight, he hit his second shot onto the green of the par-5 ninth, leaving a putt for an eagle. After that shot, the caddy, who had been eyeing him closely and watching him make so many good swings, said, "I don't know who you is mister, but you come out here dressed like that tomorrow and we can make us a lot of money."

A Long Way to the Clubhouse

The name Henry Poe, former PGA president, came up earlier in this chapter. More accurately, his name is Henry Clay Poe. Before he turned professional he was the hottest young player in North Carolina. So when Mildred "Babe" Didrickson was asked by Pinehurst home professional Lionel Callaway to play an exhibition match, Henry Poe was selected as an added attraction to join Lionel and Babe.

Callaway was a very proper person, usually attired in tie, half sweater and plus fours. The tall handsome Poe was the epitome of the southern gentleman. Babe was just plain a lot of fun, a rough tough Texas girl who liked to cut up. On occasion her language may have raised Miss Manners' eyebrows, but she always seemed to use it in an inoffensive way. The galleries loved her as she frequently played to them and made comments that they would enjoy during competition. A large crowd appeared for the match on Pinehurst's fabled No. 2 course, which is designed as a continuous 18 holes circling back to the clubhouse. They had finished playing the par-3 ninth and the group was at the 10th tee, which is located about as far out as you can get from the start. After Poe had hit and was coming back to where Babe and Lionel were standing, he overheard her say to Callaway, "Lionel, where does a fella' take a pee around here?" Callaway's face turned crimson but he must have found a spot for her, because the match was completed and all ended happily and relieved.

Just Smell the Flowers

On more than one occasion, anyone close to the golfing world has heard Walter Hagen's motto, "I don't want to be a millionaire, I just want to live like one." There are plenty of examples to back up his statement. Here are three:

Hagen lived at the Detroit Athletic Club during the wintertime. The monthly statements to the residents had been mailed. According to club policy, bills were due to be paid by the fifth of the month, and that date had arrived with no response from Hagen. The manager called his apartment and said, "Mr. Hagen, I just wish to remind you that your account is due today. Unless we have payment we would have to post it as delinquent. Of course I don't wish to do that."

Hagen inquired as to the amount. The manager gave him a substantial number over $2,000. There was a pause on the other end of the line, and then Hagen responded with, "Post it! We'll show the son's of bitches who spends the money in this club."

Walter was invited to come to Britain in the late 1920s for an exhibition tour that was going to produce a tidy sum of money. After the British newspapers picked up on the financial arrangements, they severely criticized the American for coming over and taking all that money out of the country. Not ever wanting to be thought of as a piker, Hagen rented a whole floor of the Ritz Hotel in London, bought immeasurable quantities of champagne and wine for his friends, and then had to borrow money for his steamship ride back to America.

In the 1950s, Arizona golf was experiencing a big upgrade with the opening of the fabulous new Wigwam Resort and Spa in Phoenix. With Hagen considered one of the great ambassadors of the game, the officials for the Wigwam thought it would be a great idea to invite "The Haig" for the grand opening as the special celebrity guest. They called him in Detroit to set it up and told him they were prepared to pay him $5,000 for his services. Ever the gracious gentleman, Walter replied that an honorarium wouldn't be necessary. He would just come for his expenses. "No thanks!" was their response. "We prefer to pay the $5,000." They knew The Haig.

OBSERVATIONS AND QUIPS

At the World Golf Hall of Fame induction ceremony, Judy Rankin had just completed a tearful acceptance speech. Jackie Burke Jr. followed her. When Jackie set his papers down on the podium and put on his reading glasses he turned to Judy and said, "Judy, you got me in casual water up here."

When Jerry Pate won a PGA Tour event with an orange golf ball everyone thought it was innovative. When in fact a Golf Magazine ad in 1926 touted oriole orange and canary yellow golf balls from the Wilson Company.

How they read greens on the Senior Tour (now Champions Tour): they walk from their ball to the cup and if they are out of breath, they know it's uphill; if they trip, they know it's downhill.

Former U.S. Open and Masters Champion, Dr. Cary Middlecoff, was once asked at what point in his career he became a good player. His response, "When I learned to hit my 7-iron the distance I used to hit my 9-iron."

Walt Roessing came up with this great Chi Chi Rodriquez story. "Faced with a particularly difficult seven-foot putt, Rodriguez studied it from one side and then the other. Eventually, he turned to his caddy and asked, 'Which way will it break?'

"Citing the time-tested rule of the links, the experienced caddy replied, 'It will break toward the ocean, always toward the ocean.'

"Still frowning, the frazzled Chi Chi said, 'Which one, Atlantic or Pacific?'"

QUOTES

"I've never short-changed myself on dreams." **Tom Kite**

"If it weren't for golf, I'd probably be a caddy today." **George Archer** (Masters Champion)

"In golf, driving is a game of free-swinging muscle control, while putting is something like performing eye surgery and using a bread knife for the scalpel." **Tommy Bolt**

"Watson scares me. If he is lying six in the middle of the fairway, there is some kind of way he is still gonna' make a five." **Lee Trevino**

"I wasn't much for being an amateur. I got tired of polishing the silverware." **Patty Sheehan** (U.S. Women's Open Champion)

"The tournament professional survives by confidence and so must never allow thoughts of his own fallibility to penetrate his consciousness from any source...he has to believe in his prowess, because that faith in himself is his greatest asset." **Arnold Palmer**

"Do you know how hard it is to write 59? I have written 69 three times." **Al Geiberger** (when signing autographs after his record score)

"The same way you do." **Jack Nicklaus** (when asked how he missed a putt from a foot and one-half)

"The smart golfer always tries to hit his second shot, the mulligan, the first time." **Anonymous**

"Golf mastery is an illusion perpetuated by the occasional good shot." **Anonymous**

Students and Lessons We'll Always Remember

The lesson tee has provided professionals with some of their most interesting moments and amusing incidents. I believe after reading the following, you might concur.

BETTY GIVES ME A HAND

She was a middle-aged adult "Little Orphan Annie," sandy-haired, full of fun, athletic, and outgoing. She was also my daughter's elementary school teacher. Her name was Betty. In an age when you could still do such things, Betty kept a baseball bat in the corner of her classroom and jokingly warned the fourth grade children that she would have to use it if they got too far out of line. Everyone knew she was kidding. When she showed up at Oakway Golf Course for a series of lessons I looked forward to it, aware that she possessed some athletic talent. After an exchange of information concerning her goals, golf history, possible physical limitations (my usual first-time questions), we warmed up.

I asked her to hit a few shots with a 7-iron. Her swing was very stiff and upright, almost no wrist cock in the backswing and a powerless pushing action in the forward swing. Demonstrating just a few of these efforts to me was enough: I was puzzled. I had seen her swing the classroom ball bat, and that looked natural. So I told her to elevate the 7-iron in the air to simulate a baseball swing. I extended my right hand out a bit below what would be waist high for her and told her to swing right where my hand was. She looked at me quizzically. Keeping my hand there, I repeated the request to swing where my hand was, since I was going to remove it. Just then someone behind me called, "Gary!" I turned my head to see who it was as Betty made the swing....while my hand was still there. Yes, she did have a powerful baseball swing and my hand took the full force. It hurt like hell despite my protestations to the contrary, and I quickly put it behind my back. Betty was horrified. She apologized profusely, although it was totally my fault. Eventually we were able to finish the lesson.

Her next lesson was a week later. Betty showed up with a brown paper grocery sack from which extended a quarter-inch wooden dowel. "I brought you a present," she said. She proceeded to pull out of the sack a stuffed cotton work glove on the end of the dowel. "The next time you want to put a hand out," she explained, "use this!"

Always Humble Harvey

Galveston, Texas, was the original home of Mildred "Babe" Didrickson, one of America's greatest female athletes and a champion golfer. If that weren't a special enough reason for me to be in this Gulf Coast town, then how about being paired with Harvey Penick and Jimmy Demaret to conduct a PGA teaching seminar for Southern Texas pros? The meeting room was packed, largely because Demaret, one of golf's great storytellers, was on the program. I would guess it was probably the first time in 10 years he had come to speak at a section educational event. Harvey, of course, was also a drawing card being almost everyone's favorite teacher. He was one of the most self-deprecating individuals I

Galveston was the original home of Babe Didrickson.

have ever known—a simple, straightforward, basics teacher who employed a "Texas-sized wagonload" of homemade psychology.

Jimmy was up first to address the crowd on the subject of "teaching golf." The three of us had been given 45 minutes each to make our presentations. Jimmy started by telling stories about his experiences on tour. He didn't much waiver from that topic. Before you knew it, his time was up. Even though he didn't say much about teaching, he was great at captivating and entertaining the audience. Jimmy checked his watch and said, "Boys, I'm about out of time, but I can take one question."

An elderly professional in the back of the room stood up and said, "Jimmy!"

Demaret promptly responded, "'Buck,' haven't seen you in a coon's age. What's the question?"

Buck continued, "Jimmy, you have those great big forearms that seem to let you crush the ball. Did you ever do anything special to build them up?"

Demaret thought for a moment, and then responded. "You know, Buck, before I went out on tour I worked in the bag room for two years and had to clean up all the clubs as they came in. I guess I built my arms up that way."

As Demaret stepped down from the small stage, he received a generous round of applause while Harvey Penick, speaking second, carefully climbed the three steps to the platform. Harvey was wearing a light blue alpaca sweater that exactly matched his kind blue eyes. He turned, faced the audience, and in a soft Texas drawl said, "I reckon I cleaned about 300,000 more clubs than Jimmy Demaret ever saw." Then, while holding up his right arm and pulling his sweater down to reveal a very skinny forearm, he concluded, "And look at my arms." It was a great start.

Maybe a Bad Swing but a Good Memory

Gene Borek, perennial outstanding player and all-around good guy from the Metropolis Club in New York, told me this story about a most unusual lesson that occurred while he worked at the Fairview Club. There was a new member who was in his 70s, and he came to Gene with the complaint that he was hitting his irons to the left. So Gene said, "Let me watch you hit some."

He said, "Well, I'm hitting my irons to the left." So Borek suggested that he would like to watch the man hit a few so Gene could get an idea why.

The man replied, "They're going to the left."

Borek finally got him convinced that he needed to see the man swing. So he hit a ball, and it went to the left. He said, "See, I told you so."

Then Gene asked him, "Have you taken lessons before?"

"Yeah, I've taken some lessons."

"Who did you take them from?"

"J. R. English," the man answered.

"J. R. English! He retired from Fairview 40 years ago," responded Borek.

The man then said, "Yeah, my lesson was 55 years ago."

It was the last time he had hit a ball, but he remembered they were going left.

He Looked Good in Pink

At the Grand Cypress Golf Academy they have a number of overseas students attending their schools. Top 100 Teacher and Director of Instruction, Fred Griffin, tells of two Japanese golfers who were coming to one of their sessions. It was hard for the academy staff to discern from the names which was the male and which was the female. As Fred explains it:

We had our staff assistants make up golf gift packages for them that were delivered to their rooms. They had the same last names, and one had put down small for the shirt size and one had indicated medium. So we assumed that the small was for the wife and the medium was for the husband. But actually it was not a husband and wife, but two brothers who had come together to the school. On the first morning of the school they both came walking to the range. The one brother who had put down size small showed up in his pink ladies' visor and his small pink ladies' shirt. It was so skintight on him it looked like a wetsuit. We wondered if we should say something about it, but we decided, no, let's not make him feel embarrassed; we'll just let him go through the rest of the day dressed like that. And we did.

What Would I Have Said?

If the PGA professional who had this next experience asked me what I would have done in this situation, I don't believe I would have had a better answer. As he told it:

One of the funniest and most unusual lessons that I've ever given was to a woman who had come over with her husband to Pinehurst from Myrtle Beach. I went through my usual questionnaire. "Do you have any physical problems; how's your balance; how's your coordination; do you hurt anyplace?" All the answers I got were, "Oh, I have no problems; I'm a pretty good athlete: I move pretty well."

The woman was about 70 years old, and I didn't think she was quite as athletic as she thought she was. Anyway, I started by asking her to begin a small swing to get her body moving with me helping her a bit—"Move to the left—move to the right—and try to release your swing here at the bottom." Then I said, "Now, I want you to try this. Feel like you're turning so your weight goes over your right leg in the backswing." I got away from her and sure enough, she turned over her right leg, but as she did so she overdid it, lost her balance, and fell down. Her feet went up in the air, and I saw this thing fall on the ground beside her. I wasn't sure what it was. I picked it up and asked, "Is this yours?" She answered that it was—her wig had fallen off! Unfortunately her husband was sitting there laughing at her. All this was on videotape, which made it all the worse. The poor woman...I don't know if she's even playing golf anymore. She said she'd be back, but I never saw her again.

DON'T OVERDO IT

There never has been any argument that Gary Player has been one of the best bunker escape artists of all time. That didn't happen by accident. Player spent countless hours hitting those shots and applying strict standards on himself as to the number he must hole out before ending practice for the day. While at a Tour event, Gary was in the practice bunker when fellow Tour player Bruce Devlin, who later became a television announcer and course architect, walked by. Thinking this might be a chance to pick up a pointer from the master, Bruce asked Gary to tell him how he played the shot. Gary explained that he set his feet firmly in the sand, played the ball forward in his stance, opened the clubface a little, and swung aggressively through along his shoulder line. Then demonstrating, he did what he had just explained. He swung, the ball popped out, danced briefly on the green, then rolled right into the cup. Devlin was impressed but thought *lucky so-and-so*. He then asked Gary if he would show him again. So Gary planted his feet, played the ball forward, opened the clubface, and swung aggressively along his shoulder line. This time the ball seemed to be going right toward the hole again but lipped out at the last moment on the right side of the cup. He had almost made two in a row. Then Player turned to Devlin and said, "But you don't want to open the face too much."

Both a Master's winner and a master in the sand.

An Unusual Start and a Different Finish

For years one of the great amateur tournaments in the United States has been the North-South, played at one of the meccas of golf in the world, Pinehurst Country Club in North Carolina. The list of winners looks like a Who's Who of Golf in this country. This story concerns the oldest winner of that event, Mr. Tom Draper, who captured the title when he was 51 years of age. A huge man with an equally huge reputation for winning golf events, he was once picked by the immortal Sam Snead to be Sam's partner in a short-lived event, the National Pro-Scratch, where one pro and one amateur competed on a better-ball basis against the field.

Tom told me a story about the second year of the tournament with Sam. "We were on a par-3 hole. I had pulled my iron shot into the left bunker. It was the result of coming over the top, a swing mistake I had been making for a long time. I went back to where Sam was standing and asked him, 'What am I doing wrong, Sam? Why do I keep coming over the ball?'

"He looked at me and said, 'Help your own &$#@* self. Nobody ever helped me.' And he was my partner for two years!"

Years later, when Tom was in his 70s, he called me at my home in North Palm Beach for a lesson. It is always a thrill to spend time with a nationally known competitor in an attempt to help him with his game, so I was happy as we rode out to the practice tee in a golf cart. Before I could get the clubs and my teaching aids out, Tom handed me a letter-sized piece of paper folded into quarters. I unfolded it and saw a long list of items, numbered from 1 to 14. Tom explained, "This is a list of 14 things I've tried to stop from coming over the ball. None of them work, so don't try any of these." That is an unusual way to start a lesson, but as it turned out, there was to be an unusual way to finish it as well.

I asked Tom what his problems were and what he wanted to get from the lesson. His answer was not unexpected. "I'm getting no distance and I'm still pulling my irons." Well, those two problems are closely related, so I already had some thoughts in mind when we started. I suggested to Tom that he loosen up first with a wedge and then we would start by hitting some 7-iron shots. The warm-ups were okay, kind of a half swing with a mostly hand and arm follow-through, yet guided by experience to stay on line. The full 7-iron shot was something else…or rather it wasn't something else. That is, the backswing was the same length as the warm-up wedge, to about hip height, and the distance he got from the shot was way too short. He hit both thin and heavy shots and at least half of them were pulled. Tom had little to no rotation of his hips and trunk back or through the ball. I asked him to lengthen the backswing. He couldn't—the flexibility wasn't there. It was time to stop.

"Tom," I said, "You don't need a golf professional, you need a gym and a physical trainer. I know what should be done to add length and to keep you from coming over the ball, but your body won't let you do it. We are going over to the fitness center where I'll show you some exercises that will allow you to take advantage of instruction. Until then, being here is wasting your time and money." So that's what we did. Tom was obviously very strong, but his range of motion was terrible. That's where we focused. The session was soon over. I called him in a couple of months to see if he was doing better. He indicated that he was improving. The lesson should be clear: No matter how much you know about the game, it still is an athletic endeavor; to do it well requires a body trained to perform the task.

SAM SOFTENS UP

Just so you don't think that Sam Snead was always as hard-hearted as it may have seemed to Tom Draper, there were signs that he softened up in his later years. One great friend of Sam's with whom he played a lot of golf was Lewis Keller, a fine amateur golfer originally out of Texas and later in his career the owner of Oakhurst Golf Links near White Sulphur Springs, West Virginia (Oakhurst is the oldest course in America and unique in that when you play the primitive nine-hole links, you do so with 1890s style equipment, including a gutta-percha ball. It is a marvelous and authentic throwback in time). Anyway, Lewis had played innumerable matches against Sam over the years, always for a little wager. Keller said, "In all those years Sam never gave me a lesson or a tip on my swing. A few months before Sam died we were playing at the Homestead. After I had hit a poor shot Sam came over and said, 'Lewis, you know what you have been doing wrong all these years?' It was the first time he helped me, but we were always great friends."

Sam mellowed later in life.

An Impromptu Lesson

The women's golf group at the Club Med Saints and Sinners Courses in Port St. Lucie, Florida, loved to receive PGA pro Greg Cerulli's tips before they teed off each Tuesday morning. One reason was that they were always fun. On this particular Tuesday, the day of this story, he again didn't disappoint them.

Greg is a very good player. He is also a funny guy to be around—everybody loves his sense of humor. It was 7:50 a.m. when Greg was walking through the clubhouse on his way to the 8:00 ladies' group where he was to give his swing tip for the day. At that moment he had no idea what he was going to do. He needed inspiration. As he stepped over the vacuum cleaner hose that the cleaning lady was using, he got that inspiration. "Let me borrow that section of hose for just a few minutes. I'll bring it right back," he said. The clubhouse had one of the built-in central vacuum systems where you simply attached the hose to the wall at different locations in the room. The fitting that went into the wall unit was a metal turn handle with two pro-trusions to aid one's grip. The tube itself was the expandable coil type. With the weight from the metal on the end, Greg envisioned the perfect centrifugal force swing device. He took a section of it to the range where his expectant audience waited.

After an opening golf story and a brief explanation of how centrifugal force worked in the golf swing, he began his demonstration. Starting with a small swinging motion, Greg gradually increased the swing, which was accompanied by a "whoosh" back and a "whoosh" through. Longer and louder he swung the hose, until he turned on the full force with the weighted end zipping around his back and coming up to hit him in the center of the forehead. It nearly knocked him down. His head was bleeding and his audience was ready to mother him. He stoically declined medical attention, instead pointing out the tremendous power obviously available when using centrifugal force.

First Things First

Harvey Penick was such a practical teacher—nothing fancy, no big theories, and no unnecessary words. When he felt the critical point was made during a lesson and the pupil had it, the lesson was over. One of his most dedicated students came all the way from the East Coast to Austin, Texas, to take a lesson on how to get out of a bunker. Harvey protested from the outset that she needn't come all that way just for a bunker lesson, that there were lots of good teachers in Florida who could handle the problem. But his prospective pupil persisted. Soon she was in Austin heading out to the practice tee with Harvey, who carried a bag of practice balls.

She said, "Mr. Penick, the practice bunker is over there. I want you to teach me how to get out of the bunker, remember?"

Harvey continued undeterred toward the tee then said, "First I've got to teach you how not to get in 'em."

Actually He Was Right

When I first arrived in Eugene, Oregon, to start my doctoral studies, I was assigned to teach a golf class as a part of my fellowship responsibilities. The class met twice a week at Oakway, one of the local public golf courses, where the students could use the range to practice. While I enjoy group instruction, this class was quite large, 34, which severely limited my opportunity to spend individual time with the students in the 90-minute period. Probably because of this, one of the students approached me after a class session and asked if a fraternity brother of his, a varsity golfer, could come to a class session and give him some help. When he told me the golfer's name, I was more than agreeable; he was number one on the Oregon golf team and possibly the best amateur in the state. He was also a fine young man.

At the next class, my student's friend, John, showed up to offer some help. After the group warm-up and some instruction and drills given by me, the class started hitting 7-iron shots. I began my observation and coaching from the middle of the semi-circled group, working down the line to the left. John and his friend were ahead of me and within listening range, so I could hear their conversation. The student made some good practice swings and then stepped up to a ball. He produced another good swing, but his head came up just enough so that the club couldn't quite make solid contact with the ball and he topped it about 50 yards out in front of him. Watching the swing from behind, John immediately identified the problem and said, "You topped the shot because you lifted your head. Don't raise your head up on the next one." The student made a couple more good practice swings, obviously trying not to raise his head, then stepped to a second ball, swung and topped it again, almost the same distance. This time, however, his head stayed down, but his left arm bent and shortened its length near impact, producing a near clone of the first shot. John was right on it "You've got to keep your left arm straight. Don't bend your left arm." Now our student's practice swings started to become more stilted. His mind was obviously on what he *wasn't* supposed to do. He stepped up to another ball, paused for longer than he should have, then made a rather awkward attempt at a swing with a straight left arm and a lowered head. These requirements stopped his forward motion so that he hung on his back foot, swung up rather than down on the ball, and topped it again about 50 yards. The mistake (lack of weight transfer) was immediately picked up by John and communicated to his friend, but it was too late. *Don't raise your head, don't bend your arm, and don't stay on your back foot was not going to get it done.* The swing was gone. What is of interest however is that John had a great eye. Everything he saw and noted to his friend was correct. It is just that there is more to teaching than simply revealing the right or wrong mechanics. John was a great player, but there is a great deal more to know to be a great teacher.

JUST A LITTLE MORE SPEED

The Everglades Club in Palm Beach is quite a place. It has a "Who's Who in Worldly Goods" kind of membership and the word "posh" may have been invented there. An employee at the club once decided to take a picture of each different Rolls Royce in the member parking lot. When he reached 22, he figured that was enough.

They don't have a junior golf program at the Everglades Club, but they sure are heavy in senior seniors. Someone jokingly said they used to get into some of the older members' lockers and take the spikes out of their shoes to save the greens from those who shuffled across.

One of the fine golf professionals they have had over the years, Bob Moser, shared this with me when we were out together with our wives for dinner.

> I may have set a world record today. I gave four lessons this morning and the average age was 83. The last lesson was with a lovely woman, accompanied by her husband who was close to 90. He was quite hunched over and walked with the use of a cane.
>
> "Bob," the husband said, looking up to the pro, "You gotta' help my wife."
>
> "What's her problem?" I asked.
>
> "No distance!" was the answer.
>
> So after some preliminary exercises and practice swings, I teed one up so she could hit a drive. The swing was so

slow that it was the first time I ever saw the club head bounce back after it struck the ball before following through. It seemed like a grand super slow-motion camera was recording impact. I managed to get her a little more distance and everyone was happy. But those first swings were sure slow.

He Got His Attention

There was a teaching professional in Florida who served at one of the military bases. He was retired military himself. It was a busy place, with many personnel retired from active duty living in the area. It had been a long day of teaching. His final lesson was with a retired general who was fighting a slice. The professional gave the general a couple of anti-slice moves and positions but to no avail. The moves and positions normally worked, but the general just couldn't seem to produce what was being asked of him. Every ball was a banana out to the right side of the range—"slice city."

The professional finally lost his patience. He felt the general wasn't focused on what he was presenting, so said, "Give me your keys!"

"What?" asked the general.

"Give me your keys!" the pro repeated. The general reached into his golf bag and retrieved the keys from one of the pockets. They were the keys to his beautiful silver Cadillac that was his pride and joy. He had his car washed and waxed every week and drove it with obvious pride.

The professional walked away with the keys saying, "I'll be right back." The next thing the general saw was his car being pulled onto the range, right where his sliced drives were going. The pro returned and said, "Okay, now hit it like I told you to." That got the general's attention.

It's Not a Game of To

Without question, the single best tip I ever received for teaching and playing the game came from a fellow professional, Toney Penna. Penna was primarily known for his club-making abilities, having been instrumental in designing clubs at MacGregor when they were the best in the world. Later he founded the Toney Penna Company where he continued to make fine clubs for the trade. He was truly an artist in the grand Italian artistic sense. Toney was a protégé of Tommy Armour, who always counseled Penna to keep things simple. That was evident in Toney's classic club-making designs. But Penna was also a fine player, having defeated the reigning champion Ben Hogan in an early round of the 1947 PGA and finishing among the top 20 money winners five different years while on tour. His playing ability translated well to his teaching prowess, although he had little time to give lessons.

Through the ball in Japan, just like Penna said.

Penna and I were playing a friendly round at the old PGA Country Club when billionaire John D. MacArthur was still "the man" (he owned the facility) and before it became JDM Country Club, then later Ballenisles. After we finished the 18th hole, Penna took me aside and gave me a simple tip that has been the most honest and useful of all I have been exposed to. "Gary," he said to me, "Golf is not a game of *to*. Golf is a game of *through*."

So picture with me the examples of where that holds absolutely true. You are putting at the 18th for the win, a straight five-footer slightly uphill, and your hands tighten as you swing the putter head *to* the ball rather than stroking *through* it. The putt comes up two rolls short of going in. The culprit here is deceleration caused by tension that comes from introducing the ball. When you make a practice stroke or swing and no ball is there, you always finish with a flowing *through* swing or stroke. But with the ball in our sight, sitting there saying "hit me, hit me," we try to do just that, adding muscular tension to our hands and arms, which kills speed or flow.

For other examples consider these: When you find your ball in the bunker and play *to* it, you decelerate, failing to deliver enough energy to the shot and consequently are unable to exit the bunker: With a chip shot you chunk it; with an iron you hit the turf first; with a wood you push short and to the right, or hit a quick low hook. The litany of errors is lengthy when you consider the absence of a singular fundamental, *through* not *to*.

Golf's Golden Steps

From the years 1991 through 2001 it was my privilege and pleasure each year to make a short golf presentation on the range at Omaha Country Club for the Warren Buffett, Omaha Golf Classic. I really don't like to give a golf clinic that deals with swing mechanics to a group of players just before they tee off. The game is hard enough without a player trying on the course in competition something he or she has just heard but never practiced. Instead, for most of those 10 years I would bring some of my antique golf collection, demonstrate the old clubs, tell historical stories, and give one or two simple contemporary tips that usually related to the short game. But on occasion we'd throw in something on the full swing. Here are two examples.

It is very hard to find golfers who would not like to get more distance from their drives. So in 1997 at "The

Warren Buffett and the author in Omaha.

Buffett," as we liked to call it, I told the group that we were going to give "the secret to distance." Actually, I had written my doctoral dissertation at the University of Oregon on that very topic. It was titled, "Human Factors Influencing the Golf Drive for Distance," so the "secret" idea wasn't so farfetched. First, I demonstrated "Golf's Golden Steps" by walking ahead on the range for about 10 yards, then turned and explained that the "Golden Steps" are the ones you take past your opponent's drive. Returning to my hitting spot I then said, "But they aren't the most important steps that have been taken because the most significant ones were *small steps*, in fact *one* small step, and it was taken by one of our players today. Neil Armstrong,* raise your hand." And he did.

* Neil Armstrong, the first man to walk on the moon.

Having studied long driving and having been a long drive competitor I then said, "Here are the factors that are important. Number one, *choose strong parents.*" While this is a bit of a jest, in many ways it is not. Heredity will definitely play a huge role in one's natural ability to produce speed. I continued, "We are all given certain gifts. Beyond that you need to work on golf-specific strength, maintain your flexibility, practice speed drills, and get some good instruction. That will produce the results you are looking for."

Now I threw in a surprise. "George Brett, come out here," I said. So the all-time great third baseman from the Kansas City Royals, who was the league's leading hitter, stepped out of the crowd onto the tee area. "Now you all know what a great hitter George was and have heard also what a long driver he is on the course. So we are going to have a little driving contest that is strictly impromptu, right, George?" He nodded yes because he knew nothing in advance about what I was doing. "Okay, the rules are: one swing, one ball, and longest shot between the two trees at the end of the range. Got it?"

Being the consummate pro that he is, George stepped up and ripped one about 285 right between the trees. He smiled and looked at me with a "Chase that one, buddy," look. So I turned to the crowd, unruffled with the challenge, and said, "Now let's give George a hand because that wasn't so bad [applause]. George, sorry to 'one up' you, but I'm going to really smoke one, so stand back and watch. I just hope you don't feel bad." I took plenty of time rehearsing a mighty practice swing. Then I approached the ball, which I had secretly teed in advance, took a big cut, and the ball shot out for about 125 yards before it let out a stream of bright blue smoke. It was a smoke ball! Laughter and applause followed and George laughed as well. It was all a ruse.

The second example is from the year 2000, when at "The Buffett" I was asked to spend a bit more time on swing technique. I relented, doing and saying the following. "Today we are going to show you three things Tiger Woods does before he ever swings the club. If you pay more attention to them it will help your game. The first one is grip. Tony Pesavento, our Omaha Country Club head professional, is going to demonstrate how important that first step is."

Tony is a tall, good-looking athlete, with a beautiful flowing upright swing. I had him take a 5-iron and said to the group, "Now watch as Tony makes a swing with his excellent grip." The ball jumped off the clubface and flew at just the right trajectory with a slight draw and good length. "Now he is going to make that same beautiful swing again, but I am going to change his hand position and rotate both hands counterclockwise on the grip. Okay, Tony, let's see that beautiful swing again." This time, even with a good swing, the ball started to the right and went even farther right, a terrible push slice. Turning to the audience I asked them, "Did you see how far right that shot went?" They nodded in the affirmative. "Do you know what we call that shot?" I asked. Without waiting for an answer I told them. "That's a Rush Limbaugh shot [referring to the right-wing talk show host]. It's so far to the right." There was some light laughter in the audience, and then I said, "Rush, raise your hand so we can see you." He was in the audience, and so with a sheepish smile his hand went up.

Next, turning to Tony Pesavento, I adjusted his hands into a strong clockwise-rotated position, just the opposite from before, and again said, "Okay, Tony, let's see that beautiful swing." This time, even with the good swing, the shot resulted in a wild sweeping hook that ran off the range into the woods. Facing the audience again my question this time was, "Did you see how far to the left that went?' They nodded. "Do you know what we call *that* shot?" I asked. Again they didn't know. So I told them, "We don't have a name for it because there is no one in this group that is that far left."

Tony and I finished up with a brief demonstration of the other two elements, aim and setup, which are certainly important parts of Tiger Wood's preparation before the swing. Bringing the clinic session to a close I reviewed the three points: grip, aim, setup, and as I was letting them go, said, "Oh, one more thing. When you get out there, have some fun. But remember…you ain't no Tiger Woods."

You Really Want the Secret?

The Western Open, which used to be the equivalent of a major championship before the Masters appeared on the scene, was being played in Detroit in 1960. I was the assistant professional at the Meadowbrook Country Club, one of the city's great member courses. It was early in the week of the Western event and one of the fine players of the time, Jerry Barber, requested to come and practice at Meadowbrook in order to get away from the crowd at the tournament site. His is quite a story—he won the PGA Championship, was selected Player of the Year, and served as a member on the Ryder Cup team, all even though he was a mere 5' 5" tall and weighed but 135 pounds. When Barber arrived at our club around 8:30 a.m. he asked me to show him to the short game practice area, which I did. We were quite busy in the Meadowbrook shop that day but I did take time to notice that at noon he was still in the short game area. Jerry stopped for lunch with our head pro Paul Shepard, but then for most of the rest of that afternoon, until 4 p.m. when he went to the range and out on the course, he stayed around the short game area hitting all types of chips, pitches, lobs, bunker shots, bump and runs and lots of putts; anything that would help save a stroke.

When he won the PGA Championship the following year, he was four down to Don January with three holes to play. He sank putts of 20 feet for a birdie, 40 feet for a par, and 60 feet for another birdie to get in a playoff that he won. Many people said how "lucky" he was. But Jerry Barber was the first person I ever head make the statement that has often since been quoted, "Lucky? Yeah, and the more I practice, the luckier I get."

Stan Wood was a giant next to Jerry Barber, but Barber was a giant around the greens.

Needed the Right Colored Ball

As teachers understand, every once in a while you get a dedicated student that you can't seem to help. For me, Mark was that student personified. His problem? He could make great practice swings but as soon as you put a ball in the way, the motion would dramatically deteriorate. As many times as I would encourage him to just swing the club to a complete finish, the ball seemed to overcome the coaching and he would try to hit only with his right side and fall back to his rear foot. I used drills, demonstration, learning aids, and psychology, but we just couldn't overcome the problem.

Lying in bed one night while thinking of how I could help Mark and with sleep eluding me, I came up with a possible solution. The next week, when Mark was to have his final session in the series of six, I was prepared. I had gone to a sporting goods store and purchased a half-dozen hollow, plastic, dimpled practice golf balls. I painted them all black. Then I painted six real balls black so you couldn't tell the real ones from the plastic ones. I put them in an egg carton and when Mark arrived I took them to the range. It was demonstration time.

"Look, Mark," I started, "we have plastic balls to warm up with today. They don't go any distance when you hit them, see!" At that moment I threw one down on the concrete floor of the driving range, and of course it did not bounce. "They only go about 30 yards with a full swing when you do hit them." That was my next *come on* comment. So Mark loosened up, making some good practice swings. I placed the first black plastic ball on the tee. Believing it would not go far, Mark made a nice swing all the way to a good finish, as he had been doing in the warm-up. As predicted, the plastic ball, went about 30 yards. Ball number two followed, then three, four, five, all with good swings. Now, it was show time! I slipped in a real ball that looked just like the others. Mark made another great swing and the result was amazing, at least to him but not to me. The ball jumped off the face of the 5-iron and flew straight for about 170 yards. He was astounded. The first thing he said was, "I didn't even swing that hard." What he should have said was, "I didn't even make that much effort," because his swing did have good speed. He repeated with another ball, not knowing whether it was fake or real and we were on our way. When I am asked how he played after that experience I jokingly answer, "Great! He just has to play with black golf balls."

Just Need a Reminder

Pat Rielly, past president of the PGA and longtime professional at Annandale in Pasadena, California, once received an unusual request from a physician before their scheduled lesson. The doctor told Pat that due to his busy schedule, he only played a couple of times a year. One of those times was in the annual tournament for physicians in Southern California. The event was coming up in about a month and that's why he was taking a lesson. He only had time for this one session, so asked Pat to tape-record the lesson. The "doc" could play the tape while driving to his office or the hospital as a way of reinforcing the message from the lesson. The result was gratifying. Without practice in between, the doctor accounted himself very well at the event, playing one of his best rounds ever while focusing on what he heard from listening to the tape. It certainly demonstrates the importance of reinforcement.

EXPERIENCE...A GREAT TEACHER

With the Italian PGA as the audience, I had just completed a three-day seminar in Rome. My job had been to cover several different aspects of instruction and while doing so relate my comments to the research that stood behind a particular teaching practice. After the conclusion of the lengthy seminar, which employed translators and headphones, we were standing in the conference hall receiving and giving handshakes, Italian hugs, congratulations and the like. The organizers brought to me an elderly man and introduced him as Senor Manca, the 84-year-old professional still teaching at Aqua Santa, the most famous course historically in Italy (remains of the Roman aqueduct could be seen from some fairways). Senor Manca, who had been at the club when German generals were regularly playing there during the reign of Mussolini, did not speak English, so was introduced through an interpreter. They asked him how he liked the seminar. His response caused my heart to sink at first before it rose. He initially said, "I didn't learn anything new!" There was a pause and silence. Then he followed with, "But now I know why what I do works." Yes, science may know why, but when you are on the lesson tee for 60 years, you know how. Now he knew both.

CURE FOR A HEADACHE

I was on the telephone in the pro shop when a woman whom I did not know walked in. After acknowledging her presence and indicating I would be just a moment, I finished my call, and then said, "How can I help you?"

She replied, "I love golf, but every time I play, by the time I get home I have a terrible headache. Could it be in my swing? Would you help me?"

My next lesson wasn't due for another 15 minutes so I told her to get a wood club and an iron and meet me at the range. When she arrived with the clubs, we decided to start with her 3-wood. After the start of a promising backswing, her left arm collapsed and she completely let go with the last three fingers of that hand, causing the shaft to bang against her neck. Surprisingly, the club rebounded in her forward swing and produced a reasonable shot. I found it hard to believe what I just saw, bouncing the club off of her neck, then still being able to make the shot. I didn't comment on the technique, but asked her to hit again, and I didn't mean her neck. She repeated the previous action, letting go at the top and having the club bounce off her neck before swinging forward. The mystery really was that she seemed oblivious to this fact. The thought crossed my mind, *was it possible she was trying to create rebound speed? No that's crazy!* So after one more trial I told her, "I believe I see your problem as to why you are having headaches after golf." She didn't need aspirin, only a solid grip in the last three fingers of her left hand. I never discovered if my suggestion cost her distance on her drives. But it did stop the headaches.

END OF LESSON

One of the greatest players on the PGA Tour during the 1930s was Hall of Famer Henry Picard. "Pic" was tall, handsome, and strong, both in his physique and his personality. He left regular competitive play at age 33 due to health problems at the time, but lived to be 89. The rest of his career was occupied primarily as a club professional with a busy teaching schedule. Having been both a Masters and PGA Champion, his knowledge of the golf swing was thorough and in demand. One of his most prominent pupils was Ben Hogan. Pic got Hogan to "weaken" his left-hand grip to stop the often-devastating hook that Hogan fought throughout the early part of his career. This change was introduced while Picard was serving at Hershey Country Club in Pennsylvania. Hogan entered the next event, the North-South, and captured his first solo Tour victory. Though Picard helped some of the great players, he spent far more time teaching the average club golfer...providing they would listen.

A woman from a town about 50 miles away from Hershey arranged a lesson with Picard. When she arrived, the gracious Henry escorted her to the practice range that was located in a valley area below the clubhouse. After a very complete lesson, he

The tall, handsome Henry Picard, who helped Ben Hogan become a winner.

gave her some suggestions for practice with the plan to return in a week. The following week she appeared and again they strode together down to the practice tee where Pic asked her to demonstrate what had been suggested the previous week. She made some swings, but there appeared to be nothing that faintly resembled what had been recommended.

Picard asked her, "What are you doing, Mrs. Nelson? That isn't what we were working on."

She responded by saying, "Well when I got home and showed my husband what I was asked to do, he suggested something different and…"

She wasn't even able to finish the sentence. Henry promptly said, "It has been nice knowing you, Mrs. Nelson." He turned on his heels and headed up the hill, this time alone.

WE DON'T ALL SEE THE SAME THINGS

It was the 1960s. For a certain group of golfers, a first was about to take place. They were going to see their swings on tape at a time when video capture of golf swings was extremely rare. One reason that video was still scarce was the cost of the equipment; the other was the bulk.

The United States electronics industry was pioneering the idea of home video use. A company named AMPEX was one of the leaders. When sales for home video units didn't materialize fast enough, much of our technology was sold to Japan. They quickly became the world's largest producers of video cameras and players, both in VHS and Beta format. I was pioneering the use of video at my Eugene Register Guard Golf Schools. The notice to all of our students read, "Come and see your golf swing on television. The first time ever in the Pacific Northwest."

I set aside a time on Saturday after my morning classes for

the first "shoot." Anyone could come to have their swing shot and then shown to them. The AMPEX unit was huge. It recorded reel-to-reel on what I believe was two-inch-wide tape. The unit was so heavy that I had to have a cart built with bicycle tires on the sides to hold the recorder, player, and monitor. I took the first two people in the line, a young, reasonably athletic-looking man in his 30s and a woman about the same age who was more on the stout side. She led off while I was doing the recording: first two swings head on, and then two down line with a different camera angle. The man followed with his four recorded shots. I then rewound and cued up the woman's swings first. The three of us, plus several of those waiting their turn, huddled around the monitor to watch. The whole group was curious, since they had never seen a videotaped swing before. When the lady's four swings were shown, I asked her, "What did you see?"

These were the first words I ever got from a pupil who saw themselves captured on video: *"I see I need to go on a diet."*

Success or Failure?

Over his successful teaching career, PGA professional Ed Oldfield seemed to develop a reputation for producing great results with women students. For quite a while Oldfield was the mentor for many LPGA touring pros. But the majority of his efforts were necessarily focused on the membership at the exclusive Glenview Golf Club on Chicago's north shore where he taught.

A prominent female member with a solid 12 handicap was taking a lesson from Ed when she came up with the following questions. "Ed," she inquired, "how many years have I been taking lessons from you?"

"Well, Mrs. Thompson, I think it has been about 14 years," he replied.

She continued, "My handicap when I started was 12 and today it is still a 12. Isn't that true?"

"Yes, that is true," said Oldfield.

"I would say then, Ed, that one of us is a failure," she concluded.

Oldfield gave this response, "As I recall, Mrs. Thompson, you were 51 years of age when we began our lessons together, and now 14 years later you are 65 and still have a 12 handicap. I would say that one of us is a success."

FATHERLY ADVICE

I have always considered it an accurate statement when former Florida and Alabama golf coach Conrad Rehling opined, "Golf is the only game that has more teachers than players." Interestingly, they all seem to be male, like it is an innate part of the male gene. The fact that their handicap may far exceed their teaching knowledge doesn't deter them, especially if the victim happens to be a lovely young lady. In my experience, the most vulnerable creature in the world is a good-looking girl on the driving range. This is why, with two very attractive daughters of my own who are talented athletes, I gave them this bit of coaching. "When you go to the practice range, if approached by a well-intentioned male (whom you probably can beat) and he is offering advice, just respond with one of the following statements: 'My dad is a professional and he has asked me to limit what I am practicing to what he has instructed me.' Or, 'I will be happy to listen to your suggestions, but I charge $30 a half-hour to do so.'"

THE GREATEST MOTIVATOR

I was sitting at a National Golf Foundation dinner that was being held in conjunction with a teaching seminar at Peggy and Bullet Bell's Pine Needles Resort in North Carolina. The man seated next to me, whom I had only known for 10 minutes, had just gotten down on the floor to demonstrate his ability to do one-arm push ups at age 60. That is how I became acquainted with Paul Bertholy, PGA professional and teacher extraordinaire. Paul was then at Foxfire in North Carolina, having originally come from Sandusky, Ohio. There are teachers who are really into the game: they eat, sleep, and talk golf. But no one I have ever met was as dedicated as Paul Bertholy to this crazy, fickle, tortuous, captivating, and sometimes really fun test called golf. He lived and died by the fortunes of his students and would do anything to help them. He would get down on his knees and say to his students as he held their hands, "Now you are going to promise me to practice, aren't you?" He developed a weighted swing pipe for his students to use while practicing his specific drills. The drills taught the "rod and the claw positions" (one arm extended, the rod; and one flexed, the claw), part of the Bertholy method. He could get commitment from pupils like no one I have seen. I remember him saying, "Now on the 19th lesson we introduced the ball." That takes creativity from the teacher and patience from the pupil but Paul was a master at eliciting both. Paul Bertholy was not a student of the game; he was the equivalent of a Zen Master.

For the Teacher of Golf

I leave this chapter with a solid formula for teaching, offered to my fellow teaching professionals.

1. Build people up. Always remember, the person is more important than their swing.

2. Commit to a philosophy of lifelong learning. You may feel you know a lot now, but there is so much more that can be learned.

3. Develop a preferred teaching style, but have a storehouse of other approaches to meet individual student differences.

4. Always stay with the positive. Emphasize *Do This!* Instead of *Don't Do That!*

5. Make your presentation simple and clear. Check by asking questions to confirm if the student understands.

6. Give practice homework and motivate for compliance.

If you, the teacher, can enhance what is intrinsically good about golf; if you present it in an interesting fashion, in a comfortable setting, at a level the pupil can easily comprehend, then you are filling a role of making life more enjoyable for those whom you serve. You are contributing in part toward what some have come to call "The good life." Golf has no exclusive lock on the condition. It can be found in other places through entirely different activities. But by being good at what you do, you have met the challenge on your own turf.

A teacher who made a difference. The picture is signed by the two pupils and was sent after they had become successful adults.

Observations and Quips

I always enjoy a golf tip that's a little different. These two are from Dennis Walters, whose golf show features shots from unusual lies...not to mention the fact that he hits these difficult shots while seated in a golf car. Since Dennis had played golf normally before his accident and now plays while seated, I asked him what the most important principle is for him in making a good shot. "The most important principle for me is to park my car in the right direction," was his reply. How's that for zeroing in on the value of aim as a fundamental? His second tip is one he gives to his audience to help them get their swing path to approach the ball from the inside: "Try to make your swing come just off your right fender."

Derek Hardy, a *Golf Magazine* Top 100 teacher who now resides and works in California, started to make his reputation several years ago while working with Beth Daniel in South Carolina. *Sports Illustrated* interviewed him and asked this question: "Mr. Hardy, how is it that you can charge $480 for a series of six lessons but $1,000 for one?"

"Well," Hardy replied, "If they are going to expect a miracle they ought to pay for it."

Harry Obitz from Red Cloud, Minnesota, PGA professional and cofounder of "The Swing's the Thing," had a million sayings. One was: "You make 20 mistakes in the backswing and correct 10 of them coming forward. Unfortunately you haven't quite balanced your budget."

Manuel de la Torre, the legendary teacher from Milwaukee Country Club in Wisconsin, when asked by a student who had just hit a bad shot, "What did I do wrong?" would reply, "Why? Do you want to do it again?"

Some lessons are easier to give than others. Probably my easiest was one that I did with the straightest driver of all time, Moe Norman, the Canadian star and character. One of the 30-some golf records that he holds will attest to the straightest part. He once drove over 1000 consecutive balls through a goalpost some 200-plus yards distant. So when he came to me for advice on his swing, what he got as he hit balls for me was the following:

"Good shot, Moe," "There's another one," "That one's right at your target," "And another," "And another," etc, etc.... end of lesson.

Quotes

"Six years are needed to make a golfer…three years to learn the game, then another three to unlearn all you have learned in the first three years. You might be a golfer when you arrive at this stage, but more likely you're just starting." **Walter Hagen**

"I never became a good player until I got out of thinking too many details and learned to focus on just two things." **Ben Hogan** (He didn't tell the two)

"Golf is an awkward set of bodily contortions designed to produce a graceful result." **Tommy Armour**

"If the left arm can be induced to caress the jacket all the way, the right arm cannot stray and the action is correct." **Harry Vardon**

"The greatest fallacy in teaching and learning the game is the expectation of execution from suggestion." **Paul Bertholy**

"Some instruction has become an institution of self-awareness rather than target awareness." **Chuck Hogan**

"Tennis is murderous; you want to kill your opponent. Golf is suicide; you want to kill yourself." **Anonymous**

"When I die, bury me on the golf course so my husband will visit." **Anonymous**

"The shank, like mosquitoes, has no redeeming qualities. Hell, even a slice can be useful to get around objects. A shank is just a disaster." **Anonymous**

CHAPTER

3

Yes, These Things Really Happened To Me

Why did I choose this name for the title of the chapter?
Maybe it's because I felt people might not believe
these stories to be true. Some are humorous,
others make a specific point or have a moral,
and some may seem hard to believe.
They all are true—that's what makes them meaningful.

DON'T ASK—DON'T TELL

As the head golf professional and director of instruction at Oakway Golf Course, a busy daily fee operation in Eugene, Oregon, I ran the largest golf school west of the Mississippi there from 1962 to 1972. It was not unusual for me to see from four to five hundred people a week enrolled in group lessons.

One Thursday afternoon, around 3 p.m., I had a three-hour break before my 6 to 7 and 7 to 8 p.m. groups arrived. Rather than go home for an early dinner, I called my wife and told her that I was going out to play nine holes, then do my teaching, and I'd be home around 10 p.m. After hanging up the phone I grabbed my light carry bag, slipped on my spikes (not bothering even to tie them), and headed for the first tee. There I found a middle-aged couple preparing to tee off.

I didn't recognize them, as we had a great deal of transient play at the course. Likewise, they didn't know me. I asked if I could play along for nine holes. They consented, and I told them to go ahead and hit, as I needed to tie my shoes and loosen up. The first hole played from an elevated tee, a 515-yard slight dogleg left, par-5, which had a creek running down the right side and trees bordering the left. In those days I could reach it comfortably in two with a pair of good shots. While I readied myself, the man chose to hit from the white tees and produced a very nice drive of about 240 yards. That was encouraging. The woman, his wife, played from the red markers, which in those less gender-sensitive times were placed only five yards ahead of the whites. She also hit a good drive, almost 200 yards, and I thought to myself, *This is going to be an enjoyable round.*

Stationing myself at the slightly farther back blue markers, I made a few big practice swings, preparing to show them how a pro does it. I addressed the ball, took my stance, aimed, and made a powerful swing. While the swing was powerful, the result was not. There was plenty of club-head velocity, but unfortunately it was about an inch and a half too high, causing me to just clip the very top portion of the ball. It rolled slowly forward across the tee box, first between the white markers, then the red, until it crept over the edge of the teeing ground, rolling partly down the hill, ending up between the crest of the hill and its base.

I've never been a great fan of "mulligans," so even though it was an embarrassing start, I chose to play my so-called "drive," attempting my second shot from a most awkward position. The grass was long and I was stupidly trying to play a 2-iron out of it from a steep downhill slope. I produced another mighty swing, and this time it wasn't a topped shot; it was a horrible shank that darted obliquely toward the creek on the right but managed to just barely avoid going in.

As we walked in the direction of my ball (we hadn't reached either of theirs yet) I asked my newfound golfing companions where they lived. They said, "Wausau, Wisconsin."

"Oh, that's a nice town," I replied, having once visited relatives there. I complimented them for living in a state that had such friendly people. When we arrived at the location of my wild second shot, it was again my turn. Feeling that I really needed to "rip one" so I could at least have a short iron shot left to the green, I did "rip it," a screaming duck hook with my 3-wood, across the fairway and into the trees on the far left side. Another humiliating shot.

As we continued our walk toward their tee balls I asked the man what he did for a living. He said, "I run a wholesale lumber yard," and after a pause, he followed up with a question to me, "What do you do?"

It was decision time. Did I or didn't I have the nerve...*I didn't*. I was certain by this time he wouldn't believe me if I told him the truth, and if he did believe me he wouldn't choose to take lessons from this "so-called" pro. Therefore, we enjoyed each other's company for the rest of the round as I played under the pretense of being a University of Oregon college teacher.

Learn the Language Before You Travel

Concluding a two-week trip to Japan, my wife, Ione, and I were headed to W.A., more properly known as Western Australia—Perth, to be more exact. We were to meet up with Graham Marsh, the globe-trotting professional who has won events all across the world, to help him institute the Graham Marsh Junior Golf

Foundation. My responsibilities also included conducting a junior clinic at beautiful Wembly Range, which sits on a hill overlooking the city and one of the world's great harbors, and paying a visit as honored guests at an Aussie Rules Football Match. The football match preceded the junior clinic by a day.

Now Aussie Rules is an action-packed, nonstop, rousing kind of a rough and tumble game, a cross between rugby, basketball, and football. The spectators really get into it, backing these athletes who are the most highly trained of all of Australia's national sportsmen. At halftime large crowds lined up at the refreshment stands, which were down below our glassed-in guest spectator box. The "blokes" in their outback shorts and matching shirts were seeking a bit of thirst-quenching Swan beer, while

we were in our suits and ties, having tea and cakes. Our group was standing in a circle upstairs for some chitchat with the other guests and our hosts. As I looked around I noticed on the lapel of the manager for Trans Australian Airways, a pin that was a bulldog, the mascot symbol for one of the competing teams. During a lull in the conversation I reached over and

"All right kids, it's time to go shag the balls."

fingered his lapel, calling to everyone's attention that it must signify he is *"quite a rooter."*

The comment brought momentary silence and then a few giggles before my host said, "You have just paid our friend quite a compliment." He then took me aside and explained that in Aussie-English "rooting" is another word for fornication. *Lesson learned*, I thought.

But the very next day, with about a hundred youngsters and their parents gathered at Wembly Range, I was conducting a short game pitching demonstration with the kids participating. The Wembly staff had provided me with a speaker system so the gathered crowd could hear me announce to the kids after they finished hitting, to *"Go shag the balls."* Now if you happen to look in an Aussie-English dictionary you will find that *"shag"* and *"root"* have basically the same meaning. So, next time, before embarrassing another host, I will study my language, slang and all, before I travel.

DENNIS AND HIS MASTER MUTT BENJI

If you have never seen a Dennis Walter's Golf Show you are missing something special. Dennis is a paraplegic trick-shot performer who, prior to a golf car accident, was facing a promising career on the PGA Tour. His shows are entertaining and inspirational. During his show Dennis tells the story of his dream to become a great tournament player performing before large crowds of people. Then came the accident. He was told he would never walk again, let alone golf. Of course he is golfing again, and performing in front of those large crowds he dreamed of, at events the likes of USGA Championships, including The Open, PGA Tournaments, The Ryder Cup, and others. His powerful message is, "If you want something badly enough, and are willing to work very hard at it, you can succeed. If I can do it, you can."

During his shows Dennis uses a companion dog to help entertain the crowd. His current mutt-friend is Benji (the dog's full name is Benji Hogan), who looks like the small loveable Benji of movie fame. At one of the PGA Merchandise Shows in Orlando, Dennis was touring the aisles in his cart with Benji at his side. He pulled up next to our Golf Around the World Company booth and immediately attracted a crowd as he demonstrated the brilliance of Benji the wonder dog.

Dennis would ask Benji questions like, "What is the par for the 16th hole at Augusta National?" or "If a player bogies the second hole what does he shoot?" or "How many green jackets has Jack Nicklaus won?" For each

Dennis Walters and Benji

question Benji would excitedly bark out the correct answer, three, six, four, etc. Questions came from the audience and Benji got them all correct. Then Dennis turned to me and said, "Gary, ask Benji a question."

So I looked at Benji and said, "How many PGA Tour events has Gary Wiren won?" The dog stared back at me in dead silence…nothing. No barks, just a blank look. Benji was correct again, the answer was zero, and of course the audience burst into laughter.

IS IT A MENTAL OR PHYSICAL GAME?

It was 1978, the year Dr. Richard Coop and I, along with Larry Sheehan, wrote the seminal book, *The New Golf Mind*. It was the first left brain/right brain book ever written on any sport. The message was not only that the mind is extremely important in golf but also that golfers should learn how to use it in its most effective way because of its bilateral nature.

During that year I became affiliated with a unique enterprise called "Monday Night Tour Schools," a creation of author/entrepreneur Parker Smith. The concept was to go into the town where the PGA Tour was being played that week, rent a large meeting room or hall, and with a team of "experts," entertain an audience of golfers who paid a modest fee to attend. We had sponsors, mostly equipment companies, who contributed to a free "goodie bag" that the audience received. It was a worthy idea, people really enjoyed it, but unfortunately the project was under-funded and quietly faded away. The show usually took about two hours and featured four speakers, including a player who was competing that week.

On this particular night our playing star was Bobby Clampett, who at the time was the hottest prospect among the young lions on the PGA Tour. My turn to speak was just before Bobby, who ended the evening program. Since our *New Golf Mind* book had recently hit the market, my topic was, not surprisingly, "The Mental Side of Golf." It was a strong turnout that evening, with about 800 to 1,000 people in attendance. After they had quieted down from the short intermission, I opened my talk with the following line, *"Golf is 90 percent mental!"*

Almost without hesitation, a voice came from an elderly man standing in the back of the room. His shouted comment, quite loud enough for all in the hall to hear, was, *"Anybody who says that ain't reached their 65th birthday."* He nailed me, and he was right. I had overstated the case. And the older I've become, the more I can appreciate how right he was.

New on the Senior Tour

One month after I had turned 50, the Boca Grove Plantation Country Club, in Boca Raton, Florida, hosted a PGA Senior Tour event. It was only 60 miles from my home in North Palm Beach. Having recently left my administrative position at the PGA of America Headquarters, I was interested in trying my wings on the playing side of the golf business. Not full-time mind you, because I didn't wish to starve, but just to get my feet wet and test myself. At the time I was teaching "Five Star Golf Schools" at the nearby world-famous Boca Raton Hotel and Club, so playing at Boca Grove would be convenient. In exchange for doing a one-hour clinic/show for the spectators the day before the tournament, I received a sponsor's exemption from my friend Jim Applegate, the golf director.

I needed a caddy. We had just the right man who was working at the hotel doing a variety of jobs. His name was "Buck" and he used to caddy for Sam Snead. Snead had been the pro at the hotel prior to the director at the time, Ron Pollane. Buck said he would take good care of me, and I knew he could because he had a lot of experience. The day we were supposed to meet for a practice round I got a note. "Dear Gary, I have me a big game over at Adios, so won't be able to make the tournament. But I got you somebody, his name is Walter, and he'll be there on Thursday...Sorry." It was signed, "Buck." You have to understand, Buck had been around. They play for big money at Adios and the caddy on the winning side can make a bundle of cash. He knew that no untested rookie was going to make much of a check at Boca Grove, especially one with no playing record...so goodbye Buck, hello Walter.

When I drove to the course on Tuesday and saw them putting up the television towers, I did not realize that what was going to happen in those towers would be significant for me later that week. It was time to register, so I entered the tournament office and was asked, along with the other professionals, to sign four golf bags for charity auctions. It flattered my ego to look at the names that surrounded mine. I then picked up my materials from the volunteers and headed for the locker room. The first two lockers were reserved for the two biggest stars in the event, Arnold Palmer and Gary Player. Player at the time was representing Boca Grove and Arnie...well, Arnie was Arnie. After that the lockers ran purely alphabetical, Tommy Aaron, Butch Baird, Billy Casper, Dale Douglas, etc. The nameplates were attractive, made of brass with the name etched deeply with black fill. As I worked my way back, Snead, Trevino, Weaver, ah yes, there it was, Wiren...but it wasn't on a brass plate. It was printed with a marking pen on cardboard. So much for flattery. Welcome to the Senior Tour, rookie!

Well, that isn't really important, I thought, *let's get out and practice*. I had no caddy yet, but managed the bag with a golf cart over to the range. My game wasn't sharp, but it was close, particularly the driving. That was largely because of my new Toney Penna persimmon driver. It was the best one I had ever owned. On Wednesday I got lucky and had the chance to go nine holes with my friend Gary Player. He kept raving over my drives as I was getting them 30-40 yards past his. I got to feeling pretty good in his company, but his upbeat personality does that to most people. I hit seven greens out of nine, but sank no birdie putts. On the holes that I didn't hit the green, the misses were only by a small amount, but failing to get up and down either time resulted in a nine-hole score of two over, 38. Player had to leave after the ninth hole, but I calculated that he had hit only five greens. His score was a two under, 34. Maybe it was then that I started to notice an important difference.

On Thursday I met Walter. He was white, meaning that he hadn't been out in the sun and didn't look like a real caddy. My first impression was that he was nervous, so I asked him if he had caddied before, and he indicated he had. But when I asked him if he had caddied in a tournament like this he replied, "No sir, this is the first time." *Great*, I thought, *it's also my first time and I don't need a beginner giving me advice. But he's here so let's go.* I ended up conducting a caddy training session before we went out for my final practice round. We managed to hook up with a group of Tour veterans that included Billy Maxwell. Billy wasn't too happy about Walter when he asked me on the fifth green, "Would you tell your caddy to quit stepping in my line!" His comment wasn't offered as a question.

On the sixth fairway I asked Walter for the yardage as I had earlier given him a yardage book and showed him how to use it. He gave me 153 yards. My 7-iron flew the green. I said, "Check that yardage again."

"I'm sorry, I was looking on the wrong page," was his answer. Great! Well at least he was sorry.

Thursday night was the pairings party. My wife and I were happy to attend, although I didn't see a lot of other players there. The tournament committee had enticed well-known entertainer Merv Griffin to be the emcee. Basically that job was to oversee the pairings draw and call out the names to see which amateurs got to play with which pros. The way they do it is to seed the pro players by their standing on the Tour and past performance. The amateur team gets to play with both a low seed and a high seed over the two days of pro-am competition; or in some cases two middle seeds. This was in the days when the professional's score for the first two pro-am days counted in the final tournament competition.

When Griffin finished the list he asked, "Who am I playing with?"

He heard, "You play at 7:38 with Gary Wiren."

"Who?" He questioned.

"With Gary Wiren, and then you play with Arnold Palmer on Saturday."

Griffin's response was…and I'm not kidding…"I'm not play-ing at 7:38 with any #@!&**/# Gary Wiren!" (Expletive, use your imagination.) He flew back to California the next day…so much for getting to play with Arnold Palmer.

Friday was my first day on tour. I arrived in plenty of time to meet Walter, hit balls, putt, try a few bunker shots, but mostly to practice my pitching, the weakest part of my game. It was finally time to go to the tee. The first hole is a relatively short par-4, which doglegs left as you near the green. My drive was perfect, long with a draw. When we got to my ball I was only 87 yards from the flagstick. "I'll take the sand wedge" I said to Walter, who had learned where to set the bag down and looked proud that he had done it correctly.

That is until he hunted in the bag for the sand wedge, and then said, "I left it back on the practice green."

Off to a great start, Walt, I thought to myself. "Go back and get it," I said. "I'll carry the bag to the green."

It wasn't exactly how I had planned to make my first Tour shot to a green. The hole on number one was cut just over the bunker, which guarded the front portion of the green, and of course I needed a sand wedge to get close. I couldn't wait for Walter without delaying play, so I took out my pitching wedge, opened up the face and hit a beautiful high arcing shot that fell just short and in the bunker. I carried the bag to the green. Still no Walter and still no sand wedge even though I was now facing a delicate shot from the sand. It had to be the pitching wedge again. After looking back for Walter and not seeing him, I stepped into the bunker, opened the face of the pitching wedge and hit a reasonable shot out to eight feet from the hole, then missed the putt. The other players finished their tap-in pars just as Walter arrived in time to carry the bag to the second tee. We were on our way again, one over par.

I soon let that pass, settled down, and started to make some good shots when a cart drove up to us on the fifth tee; it was Brian Henning, a Tour official. "Were you in the bunker on the first hole?" he asked.

"Yes, I was," I replied, "Why?"

"Because you didn't rake the bunker, that's a $250 fine."

He was right. I was hurrying to get my putter and forgot that Walter wasn't there. Whatever prize money I might win had just been reduced by that amount. *We're really off to a good start here,* I thought to myself. It was apparent that I'd better play well just to cover the fines. Fortunately, my luck started to change. I made some birdies and before you know it, my name was on the leader board in red numbers right along with Palmer and Casper who were at two under. My team was one of the groups starting in the afternoon and television was picking up the late times. I was on the 14th hole when announcer Bruce Devlin zeroed in on me hitting a 9-iron to the two-tiered green. The flagstick was located on the lower level on the right. My shot went to the upper level on the left. While he complimented the fact that I was off to a good start, he noted that the iron shot "left the rookie with a very awkward putt that he'll be lucky to get down in two." I holed it from 40 feet, down the hill and with a big break! That got his attention. However, a couple of bogies coming in dropped me back down the leader board and barely kept me in red figures. Then I reached the 18th tee.

Alongside the left of the 18th fairway, a "shortish" par-4 is an orange grove, probably part of the original plantation; on the right was a lake. I played safe (I thought) and hit a 3-wood…a pulled 3-wood. Better than in the water but right on the edge of the orange grove. I had a shot, a punch 9-iron over the water that guarded the front of the green. I just had to keep it down so I wouldn't hit any overhanging branches. I didn't. That is, I didn't keep it down. The ball ticked the lowest branch and dove into the water. I walked forward to the hazard, took my two club lengths of relief and dropped a ball, keeping the water between the green and me. That's when it happened. I tightened up and shanked the next one, also into the water. A very nervous pitch shot onto the green followed the drowned shank. Two putts later it added up to a quadruple bogey, eight. My name promptly left the leader board and did not return the rest of the week. The funny thing is, it all happened so fast. That was in October. By December I had started to forget about my crash on the course until the Christmas cards came, and several said, *"We saw you on television."* And that is how Walter and I debuted on the Senior Tour.

CHOOSE YOUR PATTERN

One of my joys of collecting golf artifacts is to find old golf balls with unusual markings. The variety would amaze you. When gutta-percha, a rubberlike substance, replaced feather-stuffed balls in the mid-1800s, they were first produced perfectly smooth. It was quite by accident when it was discovered that nicking or marking the ball improved its flight. As ball manufacturers increased in number, so did the variety of patterns of marking the balls. There didn't seem to be a great deal of rhyme or reason behind the various patterns except that by the late-1890s the bramble or reverse dimple (or pimple) was by far the most popular. An English aerodynamics expert tested balls with his homemade catapult that could throw a 12-pound rock a quarter of a mile and concluded that a golf ball would fly straighter and farther if it had less prominent markings than the pimple or bramble. Additional tests were performed concerning its putting accuracy. Balls were rolled down a leaden trough into a billiard table. Though rolled down the middle of the table, some of the bramble balls came near finishing in the corner pockets.

When the bramble lost the favor of the general public, the

market was flooded with balls marked with circles, triangles, crescents, airplanes, stars, squares, irregular mesh, and quite an assortment of dimple patterns. Among those dimpled spheres from the Spalding portion of my collection are the Midget Dimple and the Baby Dimple. It is no wonder the dimple won out. Who would ever have wanted to play a "Baby Pimple?"

Part of the author's historic ball collection.

The Problem With Caring

One of the best rounds I ever played was after having returned from a conference at The Esalen Institute, Michael Murphy's coastal California haven for the mystically hungry. There I had been part of a planning group working on "Golf in the Future" and how it could be enhanced. After having been totally immersed in the concept of "process over outcome" to improve performance, I came back to the PGA National Champion course with the attitude that I could care less about results, and shot a 66. It didn't last more than a day before I started to "care" again and was back to 75.

Mr. Gaines Keeps Me Cool

It all started in 1992. A magazine writer who was interviewing me asked a question that prior to that moment, I had never stopped to consider. "You have been involved extensively in athletics throughout your career. What is your last sports goal in life?"

I thought about it for a bit, and then answered, "To go out like I came in."

"What do you mean by that?" he asked.

My answer was, "I want to go out carrying my bag, just like I did when I played as a kid, but I want to do it in the U.S. Open."

The interview was over, the magazine was published, and the question was forgotten—until 1994 when I won the local qualifying spot for the U.S. Senior Open. It was being held in Pinehurst, North Carolina, on the fabled Donald Ross design, the No. 2 course. My response to that question from two years earlier came back to me. *"Go out like I came in."* When I got home from the qualifier I called Don Padgett, past PGA President who at the time was Director of Golf at Pinehurst, and told him the following. "You may not believe this, Don [he once called me the worst putter he'd ever seen], but I just qualified for your Open and I'd like to ask you to get me an experienced caddy who can read the greens. He doesn't have to be young and strong because I am going to carry the bag!" That is how I came to meet Mr. Fletcher Gaines.

Fletcher was an institution in Pinehurst. Everyone knew him, which is quite understandable when you consider he'd been carrying golf bags there for 47 years. Some of those loops included players like Tommy Armour, Ben Hogan, Frank Stranahan, Julius Boros…in other words, most everybody who was anybody that played there. Now he was caddying for Gary Wiren. Not quite the same. Only months before, Fletcher had been featured in both *Sports Illustrated* and *Golf Digest* magazines. I had not. He was an amiable, small, round-faced man with a great smile, and what I had hoped for most, an intimate knowledge of reading the Pinehurst greens. Best of all, Fletcher liked to tell stories. In so doing, he kept me relaxed while we played.

It was fun to be with Fletcher because as we walked down the fairways, me carrying the bag and him with the white caddy uniform and a towel around his neck, the people would holler, "Fletcher, where do you get a job like that?" He would just break out in his huge smile as I hiked on with the bag. Part of the reason I was carrying it was because of the interview for the story. The other part was that I was trying to make a statement for fitness in golf. A few of the players were grumbling because they couldn't use carts like they were allowed at their regular Senior Tour events. My position was, not only will I walk, but also I will carry my own clubs. I believe that a person's fitness level should be a part of the challenge of competing in the event when it is a national championship.

Our caddy-player relationship with me carrying was enough

of an unusual occurrence that Brent Musburger and Steve Melnyk of ABC Sports called Fletcher and me into the trailer for an interview after the first round. When Fletcher was asked if he had ever had a caddy assignment where the player carried the bag, he said, "No sir. This is the first time." He also said he was going to pull me through, which he did, as we made the cut and played 72 holes. So I became the first player in the history of the U.S. Senior Open to make the cut, walk, and carry his own bag.

Here are two stories Mr. Fletcher Gaines told me as we played those rounds:

> I had the bag of Mr. Billy Joe Patton in the North-South Amateur Championship. Now Mr. Billy Joe, he almost won the Masters one year, so he is a favorite to win here. It is the first round and we are playin' somebody we never heard of. But after 18 holes it is all even, and this man is takin' us to extra holes. We halve the first and the second, but on the third this man hits it down the middle and Mr. Billy Joe hooks it into the bunker alongside the road that's comin' into town. Just as he is settling in to hit his shot, a car pulls up and a lady gets out and says, "Excuse me, mister. Do you know where I can get a room in this town?"
>
> Mr. Billy Joe looks up at her and says, "Ma'am, if I don't get this ball on the green, you can have mine."

Fletcher also shared the story of the friendly money match with Tommy Armour and Frank Stranahan. Stranahan was possibly the most desirable eligible bachelor in America. He was a U.S. and British Amateur Champ, son of a millionaire out of Toledo, Ohio, with a knock-em'-dead handsome look about him, all accompanied by an Adonis body developed from some serious weightlifting. His opponent, Armour, was one of the world's greatest long iron players and the winner of the British and U.S.

Opens as well as The PGA Championship. They were playing the fifth hole on Pinehurst No. 2, a long dogleg par-4 to an elevated angled green that was very hard to hold. As Fletcher told it, this is what happened:

> Both Mr. Stranahan and Mr. Tommy drove it out there, 'bout the same. Mister Tommy played first and hit it on, a good shot. Then Mr. Stranahan, he played his shot and it's about 15 yards short. He comes over to Mr. Tommy and said, "What'd you hit there, Tommy?"
>
> Mr. Tommy said, "I hit a 3-iron, Frank."
>
> "Well I hit a 3-iron, too," said Mr. Stranahan, "and I'm 15 yards short."
>
> Then Mr. Tommy said, "You may be the *King of Muscle*, Frank, but I'm the *King of Iron*."

IF THE SHOE FITS IT DOESN'T MAKE ANY DIFFERENCE

There is a postscript to the Senior Open at Pinehurst. In coming to the tournament I wanted to be prepared for any possibility during the four days of the event and the additional practice rounds. Therefore, I brought four pairs of golf shoes with me, all new pairs of a well-known brand, which went into my locker. On opening day of the tournament I earned the early-bird starting time, first off the tee. You earn it by not having playing credentials that would provide you a more favorable position. But it was a lovely day, I had a good pairing, and what a thrill to be competing against the best in the world at that age level, no matter what time I was starting.

The greens were firm, cut short, quick, and basically perfect. So it was easy to notice the spike marks that were showing up on the greens, but where were they coming from? We were the first group. It was then I discovered *my shoes* were pulling up little tufts of turf on the greens when I walked across them. I started to walk more carefully, but apparently not carefully enough. By the fourth hole Tom Meeks, the tournament director, came out to our group and said he had a report of someone making spike marks on the greens. I told him it was I but since I wasn't dragging my feet, it must be the shoes. He asked if I had another pair and I told him I did in my locker. Meeks called in to have someone get into my locker and bring out another pair.

Sitting on the bench at the seventh tee, I changed into another pair. But they also brought up spike marks, so I changed again, this time into pair number three at the 10th tee and, believe it or not, pair number four at the 13th. I had used up my supply in less than 18 holes, and none of them worked to the green's satisfaction. When I came off the 18th I saw Tom Meeks again, who I knew felt like I was doing something funny with my feet. I took off pair number four and made him put them on and walk on the practice green to prove it was the type of spike in the shoes and not me dragging my feet. His short walk brought up spike marks too. And yes, I was asked on television about the shoe incident and all I could say was, "I think I also set a record out there today for most shoes worn during a single round."

HAVING FUN WITH SPEECH OPENINGS

Here are three speech openings that I have used while talking to a golf gathering. Imagine you are now the audience…

"I have a rule. Never tell golf jokes to a real golfing audience because invariably they have already heard them. Even before the Internet, if I'd hear a golf joke in North Carolina one week, the next week while in Switzerland I would hear the same joke, only with a different accent. It's as if the jokes had been sent to all golf courses and then posted on the club bulletin board. So this evening, for all you knowledgeable golfers, I will not tell any of the jokes with the following punch lines:

#1. And as the funeral procession passed he took off his hat and said, 'We would have been married 42 years today.'

#2. Or, 'Oh He is Jesus Christ, he just thinks he's Arnold Palmer.'

#3. Or, 'Then the gorilla lined up the putt and hit it 350 yards straight off the green.'

#4. Or, 'No, last time I tried to hit that shot through the barn door I got a triple bogey.'

#5. And finally, 'And the bad news is that St. Peter says your tee time is at 10:30 a.m. tomorrow morning.'

"Now if you don't know 'The Rest of the Story,' you won't have to listen to Paul Harvey to get it. Just ask your home professional, because he has heard these stories and many others over and over and has had to laugh each and every time."

I was in Tuscaloosa, Alabama, "Home of the Crimson Tide." The great Paul "Bear" Bryant, coach of the mighty football powerhouse, was still at the helm. Bryant could have run for senator, governor, or president and gotten elected for all three in Alabama. I had come up from Florida where the former Miss America, Anita Bryant, had recently been appearing regularly on television as the spokesperson for the citrus industry in that state. The ballroom in Tuscaloosa was packed with "Dixie Section" professionals when I opened with this line. "It's great to be in Tuscaloosa, home of the Crimson Tide. You know Bryant is a big name even down in Florida. [pause to accept a smattering of applause…then] *If it weren't for Anita Bryant, we couldn't sell any orange juice."* There was some good-natured booing after that start.

The author opening another speech.

I have been able to catch the audience a little off guard by occasionally by opening a golf talk with this observation: "If we have any history buffs in this golfing group you are probably aware of the 'Ascetic Movement' that gained many followers during the Middle Ages. Ascetics were deeply religious people demonstrating to God their commitment to humility. They would wear hair shirts, self-flagellate, or even lick the floor to demonstrate their humbleness and utter mortification. We don't have 'Asceticism' in our culture anymore. We don't need it...*we get the same thing from GOLF.*"

It Was Like a Machine

Many enjoyable moments of my golfing life were spent with the National Golf Foundation at seminars for teachers and coaches. One of them was at Lake San Marcos in California. Squeezed into our schedule over the third day's lunch hour was a visit to a nearby golf equipment company, Golfcraft, now long gone but then still successfully run by the late Ted Wooley…what a nice man. We toured the plant carrying our sack lunches, munching when we could. At the end of the plant tour was a demonstration of their club-testing machine, the first I had ever seen. The engineer would place a ball on the tee, set the club to a square position, engage the power, and send a 270 yard drive (long in those days) right down the middle of the range. The machine made kind of a chugging sound as it took the club away in the backswing; chug, chug, chug, chug, chug, gradually getting to the top, followed by a rapid forward swing, a release, and the "crack" of the ball. The Golfcraft engineer could set the machine to hit it farther, make it draw or fade, go low or high, whatever. I was mesmerized watching it. I didn't even realize that the rest of the group had left me and they were honking the car horn on the other side of the fence to get me to hurry up so we wouldn't be late for the afternoon tournament.

Well, we were late…almost. Driving into the country club's parking lot near the 10th tee, I found someone in my foursome was hailing me to get my clubs as they were teeing off. My equipment was in the car, so I hurriedly slipped on my golf shoes, grabbed my bag, and rushed to the nearby tee. Most of the players in the nine-hole event were around the tee when I stepped up. The 10th was a very short but tight 325-yard par-4 with a fast running fairway. The picture and sound of the Golfcraft testing machine was still vivid in my mind. After a couple of practice swings I addressed the ball and went, chug, chug, chug, chug, "crack." The ball left the clubface as if on a long string. My drive rolled onto the fringe of the green over 300 yards away. The people who had been on the plant tour stared for a moment and then said, "That looked just like that machine." It may have been true because the image was that powerful for me.

Of course I am asked, "What happened after that?"

"The usual," is my reply. "I tried to hit it 10 yards farther and the machine malfunctioned."

THE CONSPIRACY THEORY

George Johnson was an amiable Swede and one of our best players at Oakway Golf Course. He practiced a lot to earn his three handicap, but at age 63 it was starting to erode. George's practice was done in the old style, bringing his own balls in a shag bag. He'd hit them out, pick them up, and sometimes repeat that three or four times during his self-improvement sessions. That system worked at our facility because we had an area where you could still hit your own balls.

It was a warm day in the summer, and George had been on the range for a while. I was behind the pro shop counter when he came in with his shag bag, obviously very upset. He dropped the bag on the floor, hit the counter with his fist, and said in an angry voice, "What is it?"

I said, "What is what, George?"

"You know, the secret," he said. "You guys in the PGA recognize that there are six things that a fella has to do to hit the ball well, but you will only tell five. I want to know…WHAT IS THE SIXTH?"

He was serious. It must have been a really bad day of practice for George to be that upset that he would ever consider conspiracy…But even with his pleading, I never told him the sixth.

SO MUCH FOR TRYING

From the time I was a junior golfer I could hit it pretty well from the tee. In this case, "pretty well" doesn't mean pretty straight, it suggests pretty far. A hint of what was to come started at Spring Lake Park, the little nine-hole "muny" in Omaha, Nebraska, where I grew up. I was sitting on the ground near the tee of the opening hole as part of a group of 12- and 13-year-old junior golfers, watching a demonstration by the first real golf professional I had ever seen, Stanley Davies of the Omaha Field Club. Mr. Davies was originally from England. This you immediately knew, for he sported plus fours, a short-sleeved sweater, a white shirt and tie, all accompanied by a lovely English accent. I will never forget his major coaching point, nor the very proper voice that delivered it: *"Golf is like a waltz—back and through, back and through."* As he said this he made the most beautiful Percy Boomer "turn in the barrel" kind of repeating swing. It looked so graceful that it *was* actually like a waltz when he did it. He was hitting a little draw shot, about 190 yards with his 3-wood, one right after another. Then he said, "Let's see one of you lads try it now," and he pointed to me. I had my clubs beside me, so I pulled out my driver, teed it up, took my closed-faced caddy grip, spread my feet apart, and took a wicked cut. The ball carried in the air about 20 yards beyond his. He quickly took the driver from my hands and abruptly said, *"That's not the way you do it!"*

After I reached high school and later college, when playing golf the par-5s were my favorites because there were a lot of them I could reach. When I became an assistant pro at Meadowbrook Country Club outside Detroit, I spent an inordinate amount of time trying to drive the first green, a par-4. It was a feat for which "Chick" Harbert, the former head professional, was known. I did it occasionally; he did it on a regular basis.

Jump forward some 25 years. I was 47 years old, working for the PGA of America, and had garnered a second and third place finish in previous South Florida Long Drive competitions, usually with distances of around 315 to 325 yards. In this particular year I had been training regularly at the gym for the competition. Also, I had asked a local club maker, Don Kepler, to make me a special driver for the event. It was to be 47 inches long rather than the standard of the day of 43, extra-stiff steel shaft, persimmon wood head, eight degrees of loft, and three degrees closed. When I received it the day before the event, the club-head was still not varnished, just the raw wood.

The competition was being held on the first tee of the Squire Golf Course at PGA National in Palm Beach Gardens. I warmed up on the Champion range within view of the competition site. Trying the driver for the first time, I liked it. Mike Reynolds, then the head pro, was in charge of the competition that had attracted 63 entrants. I got there early enough to request that I be the first to hit. The reason was that one of my students was playing in a tournament nearby and I had promised I would watch some of her round. An added gallery of spectators that combined with the numbers of contestants made for a sizeable audience. The competition scene was set. Flags were planted down the fairway at a 40-yard width to define the area in play and that which was out-of-bounds. The fairway was also striped at 280, 290, 300, up to 320 yards. Officials were in the field with walkie-talkies to com-municate the re-

The 381 yard, one foot driver.

sults to Reynolds and from him to the audience. There was a favorable quartering left-to-right breeze that was encouraging for me, as I was hitting a slight fade with this driver. Six generic balls were allotted to each contestant. It was time to begin. Reynolds took the microphone, described the nature of the event and that it was a local qualifier for the National Long Driving Contest. "Now on the tee, from PGA National Golf Club, last year's second-place winner in this local event with a drive of 316 yards, Dr. Gary Wiren."

My strategy was simply to get the first ball in play, and "get on the board." I just wanted to make a good swing, because if you try to hit too hard too early and go out-of-bounds, you tend to tighten up. So I stayed loose, took my cut and hit it really flush. I heard Mike Reynolds say, "Boy, you backed them up" (referring to the officials doing the measuring).

We waited on the result for what I thought was longer than normal. Then it came over the walkie-talkie. Mike announced, *"Three hundred eighty-one yards and one foot!"* WHAT! IT WAS THE FIRST BALL! I DIDN'T EVEN TRY TO HIT IT HARD! But that was the measurement, and it was on a normal golf course fairway that was flat. I couldn't believe it.

Now if I had any flamboyance like one of my heroes, Walter Hagen, I would have turned to the other contestants, and while slipping the head mitt on my driver, said, "Okay, boys, chase that one." But I had five balls left. I was feeling macho. I didn't even go after the first one. So I thought, *I'm gonna' hit one four hundred yards.* And I tried. The results were: duck hook, another hook, a big push, a pop-up that I almost could have caught on the way down, and finally one in play that was short of the 290 yard marking stripe; five terrible shots. It took a few minutes to realize what had happened.

I had just hit the longest drive of my life when I wasn't trying to hit the longest drive of my life. I did it when I was trying to make my best swing (it won by 50 yards!).

CHARLIE NEVER THOUGHT THAT WAY

Kent Country Club in Grand Rapids, Michigan is the old-line club in town where you also find the "old-line money." It is a gracious club in an All-American City, so you can imagine that it is filled with All-American type people. Topping that list was the head professional, Charlie Vandenberg, a Midwesterner with a special sense of decency and manner. I was at Kent to do a three-day golf school as a visiting teacher, along with Charlie and his staff.

On the last day of the school we finished early enough that Charlie and I could go out to play nine holes together. It was fun, it was relaxing, and it was just what we needed. The fairway on the last hole parallels the clubhouse and the green sits just adjacent to a large overhanging balcony. As we hit our irons into the green I noticed that the balcony was filled with a large group of people, apparently attend-

Charlie Vandenberg with the author.

ing a formal wedding reception. They all seemed to be in a jolly mood as you might imagine on a wedding day. Charlie had hit a great iron shot 10 feet from the hole. We pulled our cart around the back of the green and walked to our putts. Apparently the balcony people were also our gallery, having watched the fairway shots. As Charlie was taking off his glove and getting ready to mark his ball, they shouted, "C'mon Charlie, sink the putt. You can do it!" All eyes were on Charlie.

While the putt wasn't long, it was a curling side hill/downhill challenge that required a perfect read. As Charlie surveyed the putt he walked over to me and said, "Gary, how do you handle these situations? I really get nervous. Those are all my members. What should I be thinking?"

I looked Charlie right in the eye and said, "What you should be thinking is @%*&# 'em."

He looked startled, but he walked back to his ball and rolled it in, accompanied by cheers from the balcony. The suggestion must have worked. It is just that Charlie Vandenberg would have never ever considered thinking anything like that.

Just Even Par

It was my second year at tiny Huron College in South Dakota where I completed my original undergraduate degree in English. I followed in my father's footsteps in beginning my higher education schooling, as he had attended Huron and convinced me I should "try it." After making preliminary inquiries into the University of North Carolina at Chapel Hill and the University of Miami in Florida, I did choose Huron and have never regretted the choice.

Golf is not a "big-time" sport in the Dakotas. That designation is reserved for hunting and fishing. Collegiate golf is about as remote as you can get from the "big-time," but nonetheless is on the map. Our Huron College golf squad was traveling to Brookings, South Dakota, to play at the Brookings Country Club, home of the South Dakota State University team. Our home course was in Huron Country Club. There the greens of the nine-hole facility were always kept very slow in the spring season, the time of this match. My putting stroke was therefore geared to a six on the Stimpmeter when we hit Brookings. The first hole was a 535-yard par-5 right-to-left dogleg around a lake that was a good fit for my hooking style. After a big drive I knocked the ball on the back of the steeply sloped green in two, and proceeded to stalk my eagle putt that was resting some 20 feet above the hole. Five putts later I ended up with a double bogey seven! So much for eagles; that green must have read at least an 11 or 12 for speed. I left it in a dark mood.

The second hole offered an interesting design and challenge. It was another dogleg right-to-left around the lake, but this time the yardage read only 330 yards. That must have been measured around the bend, not as the crow flies. The green sat out on a promontory and the normal play was an iron off the tee straight up the fairway to the dogleg, then a small wedge on in. But I was agitated from the previous hole. Figuring the distance to carry over the lake was maybe 260 yards and another 20 to the green, I decided to go for it. It wasn't a smart play, but that was my choice. I knocked it on and made the putt for eagle.

As we walked to the third tee, our coach, Gene Dennison, appeared and asked me, "How are you doing?"

"Even," I responded, but I didn't tell him how. I didn't think we had the time.

That Is a Tough Grind

A few years back I took an occasional dip into the world of mini tour golf. It was certainly not an attempt to increase my bank account, but rather to raise my awareness of what young aspiring professional players were thinking and doing. The Dakota Tour offered such an opportunity. One of their events I was able to make was in Watertown, South Dakota.

Now understand, most of the players on these tours are in their 20s, just out of college golf, or former assistant pros who have left their jobs for potential riches on the PGA Tour via the minis. I was an anomaly, as some of my children were older than these players. When I drove into the parking lot at Watertown to practice before the event, I pulled up next to a medium-sized motor home with an Indiana license plate that had also just arrived. Out from the motor home's driver seat emerged a slim male who was obviously a player. From the other side stepped his wife, while tumbling out the back were three kids ranging from maybe six up to 10 years of age. *Wow!* I thought, *that is a difficult way to play the minis*. I heard them discuss the day's plans that were to occupy the family while the father/husband practiced or played during the next five to six hours. He hugged his wife and kids, who obviously adored him, and he and I headed together toward the clubhouse with our carry bags on our backs, both chasing a personal test of our games and the promise of only a small purse. My new friend turned out to be a very sweet guy, a pro from Indiana, who was competing the entire summer on this tour being offered throughout the Dakotas. He was here because he had his dream of making "The Big Show," or at least finding out if he had the stuff to make it.

I don't remember our finish in the tournament, but neither of us recorded a top 10 or even near. What I do remember is packing up to leave after the final round. I was in the parking lot when the motor home of my Indiana friend pulled in to pick up "dad." The kids piled out again. This time there were not three, but five! I hadn't seen the other two on our first meeting. *He was traveling with five children!* I could go back to Florida after an enjoyable relaxing week of competition not having to worry about how I played. He was moving on to the next town with five kids and a supportive wife. I had to think, *"That's one tough grind!"*

A NO CONFIDENCE VOTE

At the Eugene Country Club in Oregon, Robert Trent Jones Sr. had just finished one of the greatest reconstruction jobs I had ever seen. ECC had always been a highly respected golf course but was showing its age and needed a facelift. So the club went for "Mister #1 Architect" at the time, Jones Sr. He did something I have never seen done before or since. Utilizing the basic existing fairways, which were bordered by towering Douglas fir trees, he placed the first tee on the original 18th green and the new 18th green on the original first tee, basically playing the course backward. The more amazing part of it was that they never closed the course during the construction. Using several temporary tees and a few greens, they continued to play in the old direction until the new layout was completed. When that time arrived, you simply were to turn around the next day and play the other way. I know it's a fact because I did it.

The new course was much tougher. It set an entirely different standard for difficulty in the whole Pacific Northwest. The course's first test was the Pacific Northwest PGA Championship in March. The field was strong, including several players who had spent time on the PGA Tour. The weather was still cool and wet, making the course play long. Jones' new challenging layout made it play extra-tough. A double tee start both morning and afternoon was needed for the large field. I was in an afternoon group so watched the scores come in from the morning rounds. The low score was 75 by former Tour regular Al Mengert, an excellent player. I started on the back nine. Through 13 holes I was one under par, obviously in or near the lead. The next hole bore a very strong resemblance to the famous short 12th hole at Augusta National. The Eugene version was also a par-3 over water with a green that was wider than it was deep, and it too had a pair of bunkers in the back. The difference was this green had two levels and was playing 175 yards, not 147 as at Augusta National. From the elevated tee with a bit of a wind blowing left to right and the flag down in the right front, I chose a 5-iron. Although the shot was hit well, the wind caught it more than I thought it might and blew the ball just short and to the right, landing on the bank and falling back into the water. My young caddy and I walked to the water's edge. It was time for a drop. Meanwhile my playing partners had crossed the bridge on the left and were standing on the back of the green watching as I dropped a second ball and prepared to hit a delicate pitch over the water to the front pin location. My cut sand wedge shot looked perfect; it wasn't. It hit the top of the bank, almost on the green, and spun back down into the creek. I dropped another, hitting exactly the same shot with the same result. I dropped another. This time, attempting to hit it harder, I flipped my right hand at it, chunking the ball and a hunk of turf into the water…that shot was followed quickly by another chunk into the water. I turned to my caddy to ask for another ball. He looked up at me and said, "We don't have any more."

One of my playing partners across the way was Lee Brune, a Spalding staff guy with a big red bag. I was playing Spalding balls and called, "Lee, can you loan me a ball?" He waited a moment then started laughing, and finally threw a ball across to me. I knocked this one onto the back of the green and two-putted for a 13! I had a strong suspicion I had lost the lead.

After that disaster and while walking up the path to the next tee, Lee apologized. He said to me, "Gary, I wasn't laughing at you. I was laughing at my caddy. When I asked him to get a ball for you, he looked at me and said in utter sincerity, 'I wouldn't give him a ball.'" That was certainly a "no confidence vote."

Untimely Advice

I taught in Japan for 20 years. I had a TV show there, wrote regular articles for their golf magazines, and did stage shows and range presentations. This is mentioned simply to indicate that in their golf teaching world I had a presence, but had never competed as a player in Japan. With no great playing résumé in America and limited tournament experience elsewhere, it could have been considered a mistake to put myself on record and tee it up against the Japanese Senior Tour players who had competed all their lives. But I like a challenge and so arranged to stay on an extra month from one of my teaching trips and enter four events in Japan. Don't ask if I was nervous; of course I was. Here I had been telling others in Japan how to play the game for years and it wouldn't look very credible if I couldn't do it myself.

At the first event I was on the practice putting green about 20 minutes before my tee time. A young Japanese male squatted down not far away and was looking up toward me. At first I didn't pay any attention, but finally I had to give a "Konnichi wa" (good day) show of recognition.

That allowed him to respond and he said in very plain English, "You're not a very good putter, are you?"

"What makes you think that?" I responded.

"Your eyes," he said. "Your blink rate is fast, indicating that you are not calm when you putt."

"Is that so?" was all I could come back with.

"Oh, yes. Good putters keep their eyes open almost the entire time while putting." And then he left.

About all I could think was, "Thanks a lot!" Here I was, going out for my first round of competition in Japan, and instead of working on my normal putting routine I was going to be thinking about having to keep my eyes wide open. I'll guarantee you, it is not the way you'd want to start.*

*So how did I finish? Three middle-of-the-packs and one top-ten with my eyes blinking all the way.

About to get some unsolicited advice.

THE X FACTOR

It was without question the greatest start of a golf round in my life and one played under the most unusual conditions. I was playing in Japan. I don't recall the course, but certainly remember the round. During my 20 years of visiting Japan I would frequently find myself there in early October, often on my birthday, the fifth. This day's play was a kind of Gary Wiren celebration tournament with golf professional teachers from the Mizuno Golf Schools that I directed, a couple of JPGA Tour players, plus a variety of staff from International Golf Research or IGR. The latter group was headed by Masaki Takemori and ably assisted by Jillian Yorke, an expatriate from England via New Zealand.

It was an early morning start. My group was to lead it off, an honorary thing, although I would have preferred to wait because it was so foggy that you couldn't see more than 50 yards in front of you. We didn't wait, though, because the tee times were totally full behind our group. So with the female caddies pointing the direction on the first hole (a par-5), we trusted and made our swings. I was playing with two school instructors and one of the JPGA tour players. All three had good swings. Finding our balls was going to be a challenge, but we all hit the fairway so the task was made easier. The caddy now indicated the line to the green by pointing where I should hit. It was apparently an uphill shot of about 260 yards. I could see nothing in front of me but a hanging gray blanket, yet I swung anyway. The contact was good, but where it was going to finish I had no idea. We trudged up the hill until my caddy found my ball about 20 yards to the right of the green, now visible from that distance. It looked like a relatively easy shot from my angle. I hit it close and made the putt for a birdie. Good start. The next hole was again fogbound, as were holes three, four, five, six, and seven. I was beginning to get a better appreciation for blind golfers. Nonetheless, without ever knowing where the green was, I birdied every one. That's right—seven straight birdies, including a chip in on the par-3 seventh.

When I holed out there from the fringe, the tour player turned to me and said, "You do this all time?"

"I wish I could," was all I could say.

Then the sun came out and the birdies stopped. How strange—but that is just what happened. I parred holes number eight and nine and went to the clubhouse for the customary lunch-between-nines ritual. When they asked my score and heard "Twenty-nine for the front," the word spread throughout the clubhouse, even among those not in our group who were waiting to tee off. As the foursomes following us came in and heard the news it created a constant flow of people coming over during the next 45 minutes to congratulate me. Putting aside my hashii (Japanese chopsticks) I headed for the 10th tee. Three pars and a birdie on the first four holes portended nothing unusual was about to happen—but it did.

On the par-3 14th hole I couldn't decide what iron to use. The scorecard said 157 yards, but it looked shorter. Nonetheless, I went with the stated yardage. I hit the 7-iron right at the flag. It kept going and going. The ball landed five yards over the green on the fly and settled in some long grass. I had been "faux yardaged"! It was a common practice at some of the older golf courses in Japan to "beef up" their scorecard by overstating the distance to make the course appear more challenging and therefore more worth joining. I made a bogey, the first of the day, and I was peeved. I probably even pouted a bit…you know, "It wasn't my fault" kind of thing. The next two holes I made a birdie with a lucky long putt, then scrambled for a par. Next came the 17th, a slight dogleg right around some woods bordered by a road. I was eight under par at the time and hoping to get to 10, which would have been my best ever 18-hole score in competition. I was the last to hit as my partners also had birdied the 16th. Maybe I was trying to show off with a big drive, or maybe I just let my lower body outrace my upper, but I hit a push fade into the woods. The trees were pretty thick so I announced a provisional. I hit that one over the road, out-of-bounds. This turned up the emotional heat from my earlier par-3 "peeve" so I said, "Let's go. We'll find the first one!" Six people searching found nothing that resembled a Titleist #2. After the five minute hunt I said, "C'mon that's enough." Three players finished the hole, and I wasn't one of them. I made a closing par on the 18th.

There were several people standing behind the green to hear my final number. "What did Wiren-san shoot?"

My reply was, "X, no score."...But it was the best start I have ever had, even if I couldn't see it.

The Lost Marker

While planning a trip to my hometown, Omaha, I came up with a creative idea. I wrote a letter to billionaire and friend Warren Buffett and suggested to him, "The next time I come to Omaha we shouldn't play at the Omaha Country Club with carts and caddies, but instead go to Elmwood Park, where you played as a kid, and where I won a junior tournament 50 years ago." Buffett returned my letter with the following message penned on the margin. "Wonderful idea, love to do it. I'll finally get to play the first and 18th holes." He was referring to his penchant for sneaking on to play without paying during his youth.

The date and time was set for a start late in the afternoon on a weekday when it would be quiet. I purchased two lightweight canvas carry bags that were from the 1940s and '50s and we met in the parking lot to switch our clubs from our big bags to the small ones. The *Omaha World Herald* had gotten wind of our adventure so there were two reporters and a photographer there to cover the non-event-event. The course professional refused to take our $12 green fee for the 18 holes, so we were ready to tee off on the short but hilly municipal layout.

On the first hole, a par-4, both Warren and I hit the green in regulation. His ball was inside my 20-footer and on my line, so I asked him to mark it. After a fumbling search in his pockets didn't produce any coins, I walked over and handed him a penny. As I did, the *Herald* photographer snapped a picture. That pic-

A loan from the author to Warren Buffett.

ture didn't make the front page, another shot of Buffett and me hiking to the second green with our bags on our shoulders did. But the picture of me handing Warren a penny appeared on the inside cover page of the *Herald* and the caption read, *"Wiren loans Buffett a penny on the first green and never gets it back."*

Our gallery of the three newspapermen followed us through three holes before departing and wouldn't you know it, Buffett made pars on all three of them. Maybe that's an indication why he is a winner. When we arrived at the tee ground for the fourth hole, a 155-yard uphill par-3, there was a foursome of women on the green. Seeing we were only two, they were polite enough to wave us on. Warren topped his shot, the first poor one he had hit, and of course it was after the journalist gallery had disappeared. I played a 7-iron onto the right fringe. The ladies wanted us to continue, so Warren hit up short of the green and then pitched it close for a "gimme." While I was putting from the fringe he joined the ladies and said, "That is Dr. Gary Wiren. He is a famous golf teacher on television." This rightfully made no impression with the four cart-pulling semi-senior ladies, and Warren headed for the next tee (he likes to play fast).

I finished out my putt and as I left the green mentioned to the four women, "And that was Warren Buffett."

One of them said back to me, "Oh, sure, that was Warren Buffett."

One of her friends leaned over and said, "Mary, THAT WAS Warren Buffett." I might not have made their day, but he certainly did.

OBSERVATIONS AND QUIPS

On a windy day when I was playing with PGA Hall of Famer Chick Harbert, he shared this advice with me: "The secret to driving the golf ball in windy conditions is this: When the wind is behind you, just try to focus on making your very best swing and solid contact. When the wind is against you, just try to focus on making your very best swing and solid contact."

I'll tell you a bad feeling in golf—walking between holes and having to cross a bridge over a freeway when your caddy, who is still holding your putter from the last green, drops it 30 feet to the six lanes below. It happened to me in Caracas, Venezuela at the Caracas Country Club. The recovery took a while but the putter suffered only minimal damage. My thanks to the Venezuelan drivers who dodged it.

At Celebration City G.C. outside Orlando I was on the first green after having been paired with a doctor and his wife from Chicago. The green was steeply sloped from back to front and surprisingly fast even for Tiff Bermuda. The wife played a nice shot to a middle pin location but ran it about eight feet past, above the hole. When it was her turn to putt, it was obvious that this kind of speed and slope when combined were unfamiliar to her. Making a firm stroke, she missed the cup, her ball going past at a rapid pace until it stopped, leaving 20 feet coming back. As she walked past the cup to her ball I heard her quietly say, "I guess that's one situation in life where downhill is tougher than uphill."…It was an astute observation.

———————

While paired with one of golf's great singers and performers, Vic Damone, I was humming and singing softly to myself as we walked up to the ninth green at Trump International Golf Club in West Palm Beach. Vic turned to me and said, "What are you doing?" I told him that while playing I often hum and sing to myself to relax. "Look, partner," he said, "I'll do the singing, you do the playing."

QUOTES

"You must work very hard to become a natural golfer." **Sam Snead**

"It's hard to hit a good 5-iron when you are thinking of a 6-iron on your backswing." **Charlie Coody**

"If God wanted you to putt cross-handed, he would have made your left arm longer." **Lee Trevino**

"Golf is a game, and as such is meant to be enjoyed. Find a way to enjoy it, or find another activity. Life is too short to do otherwise." **Gary Wiren**

The Best From My Fellow Pros

*I have been fortunate to have had many experiences in
the game but there are so many stories out there
that my fellow professionals could share with you if they
had the opportunity. The following are from that great
group of PGA Professionals who are my friends,
my peers, and in many cases my inspiration.*

GOOD GOLF STARTS WITH A GOOD GRIP

Carl Lohren, coauthor with Larry Dennis of *One Move to Better Golf* and consistently recognized by *Golf Magazine* as a Top 100 Teacher, has a wry sense of humor. It is well demonstrated in the following scenario. Carl was standing on the back of the practice tee after having just finished a lesson. One of the women members was passing by and decided to get a quick opinion on her grip. "Carl," she called to him. "Would you look at my grip?" He walked over to her and studied the two hands on the club as she demonstrated her grip. It was hardly up to Tour level standard. "How is it?" she inquired.

"What do you want to shoot?" Carl asked.

She replied, "Oh, 95 to 100."

"Your grip is fine," he answered.

She started to walk away, seemingly satisfied, then stopped, turned back and countered, "Carl, how about 85 to 90?"

"Then it's not so good," was Carl's apologetic but honest response.

Golf's Pied Piper

If there ever was a PGA golf professional in the United States who provided more enjoyment and fun for his members than William A. "Billy" Mitchell, I don't know who it could be. He told stories, put on skits, wrote funny poetry, had a secret Billy handshake, and was one heck of a player. Like a Pied Piper, he led people to joy through golf. When a member brought a guest to the club, the first thing he or she would want to do would be to say to the guest, "C'mon, I want you to meet our pro, Billy Mitchell. You'll love him." Unfortunately his family and the golf world lost William A. Mitchell way too soon when the former Met Section Professional of the Year died in his early 50s. Here is a sample Billy story.

When Billy taught people, he was full of enthusiasm about the game and wanted to inject that same feeling into them. At the conclusion of a series of lessons with a beginning female student he talked to her about the joys she was going to experience in playing golf and that she should celebrate those joys. "You'll make your first bogey and you can celebrate that; then your first par and birdie, the first long putt, completing your first 18 holes. Heck, you can even celebrate your first blister."

A week or so later, Billy was on the practice putting green when his pupil came over and told him she could now celebrate her first blister. "Oh, let's see it," said Billy excitedly as he took her hands to find the cause for celebration—but couldn't. "Where is it?" he wondered out loud.

"It's not on my hands. It's on my left wrist," she said pointing to a spot on the top of her arm just above the wrist.

"How did you get a blister there?" he asked.

"You know those score counters that you wear like a watch and push the button after each shot?" she said.

"Yes, I've seen them."

"Well, I took so many shots and pushed so many times that it caused my first blister right there," as she pointed to her wrist.

Laughter followed, along with a hug. We miss you, Billy.

The Hand is Quicker than the Eye…
Particularly at Night

John Raineri is a delightful guy to be around. He's a PGA club professional, a course owner, a good player, and he loves to have fun. One evening early in his career when he was serving as the head professional at a semiprivate Midwestern course, the workday was coming to an end. He had just gotten off the lesson tee, come into the pro shop, checked the registers out, and noted it was around 10 p.m. As he tells it:

> I walked into the lounge and everyone is in there having fun, drinking, and telling a lot of jokes. One of the local hustlers who had just come in off the golf course after 36 holes stopped me as I was walking through and said, "John, we've got a proposition for you. We're going to let you tee off from the front of the clubhouse here to the number two green [which was about 100 yards away]. If you can get down in three you're a winner. We've got whatever dollars that you want to put up that says you can't do it."

I told them I had to put the money and receipts away and get my books closed, so I would discuss it when I came back. In the meantime I was starting to kick around an idea.

One of my friends happened to be in the pro shop when I went to my office. I said to him, "Come with me. I'm going to give you a couple of Top Flight #1 golf balls. I want you to go out and put one on the number two green about seven or eight feet from the hole and the other on the number nine green on the other side of the clubhouse. Then come on in and join the rest of the group."

So I waited a bit and then went back to the lounge. I said, "What's the proposition you have here, Glen?"

He repeated the earlier challenge, "Well, you tee off in front of the clubhouse and play to the number two green. If you can make a three in the dark you win."

I replied, "Let's see. I've got about $100 here; I'll bet the hundred." And I put it on the table. They jumped right on this, covering it twice (of course the ball was on the green; there is no way I'd play in the dark if the ball were not there).

They grabbed their martinis, Manhattans, flashlights, and beer and we all walked out, 10 or 12 guys having a few laughs. They think they had me, right? Well, I got out there with my 9-iron and my wedge. I was looking toward the number two green that I couldn't see. I hit the ball somewhere in the darkness in that general direction but purposely away from the green. Everybody was smoking, drinking, and laughing, having a good time figuring they had me beat. So as they were looking around for the ball they spotted a Top Flight #1 on the green, which is what I had identified I was playing. The guys couldn't believe this! It was seven feet from the hole. So I two-putted and walked off.

Then this one guy said, "Can you do it again?"

I said, "No, better than that. I'll hit from here, by the number two green, to number nine green over the corner of the clubhouse. I've got a 9-iron with me so I think I can get there. It's probably about 125 yards and I'll bet I can get it down in three for another hundred."

"No way," they said as a chorus, "You're on!" I put the ball down as they produced a flashlight so I could see it. I hit it real clean but made sure I didn't get it near the green so there wouldn't be two balls there. The group then hiked past the clubhouse. When we arrived at the number nine green there was a ball, about 10 to 12 feet from the hole. It was another Top Flight #1. They were shaking their heads. They couldn't believe it! After two putts I made my three.

They weren't laughing so much now as they looked at each other and announced, "We've had enough. You win. We're through."

About a month later I figured it was time to tell them what really happened. So on a day when they were all in the lounge I pulled out a couple hundred dollars and said, "Guys, let me tell you something. Don't ever try to hustle a hustler, because you're going to get beat every time." I told them the real story and handed all the money back.

GOOD ADVICE

My friend Joe Innes, as nice a PGA professional as you will meet, told me an interesting on-course experience that he had with one of the Met Section's great players. He was competing in a Long Island PGA event at the Montauk Country Club. It was a 54-hole tournament: 18 holes the first day and 36 on the second. In the opening round Innes shot a good score that got him paired with Al Brosch for the final double round. Now Al had won more tournaments in the Met area than anybody. He led the U.S. Open after 36 holes one year at Merion, and he was the first guy to shoot 60 on the PGA Tour, so no question, this was a star. In comparison Joe made it clear that his own record was pretty insignificant.

During the final round with Joe Innes, Brosch was hitting his shots straight as a string off the tee. He was famous for that. Innes was out-driving him most of the time, providing he could find his ball, because he was not so straight. After 18 holes Brosch shot a smooth 72, and Innes is closer to a score of 76. In the afternoon they got to the 34th hole, a par-3, where they had to wait for the group in front to finish. So Joe attempted a little conversation with Brosch, which wasn't easy, as he was very much a "to himself kind of guy." Innes said, "Mr. Brosch, how can I learn to hit it straight like you?"

He looked at Joe through those tight little glasses he wore and said, "Sonny, do you know how to slice a ball?"

"Yes, I do," said Innes.

"Do you know how to hook a ball?" Again, Innes said he did.

"Well don't do neither." That apparently was Al Brosch's little secret.

A Late Call

If you sent a letter to "Mr. Golf," Battle Creek, Michigan, it would be delivered to Ron LaParl, who served a long and distinguished career at the Country Club as their head professional. As Ron tells it:

> I had a member at the club by the name of Bill McDonald, who actually lived in Miami, but spent three to four months during the summer in Battle Creek. He was a big booster of golf, having promoted the Miami Four Ball and sponsored the L.A. Open. He believed in doing things big.
>
> So one year he invited Ben Hogan and Sam Snead to come and play in an exhibition at our club. He paid them $2500 apiece, which at the time, the early '50s, was good money, as much as you would take home finishing high in some Tour events. McDonald was in the trailer manufacturing business and had a big trailer parked out in front of the club with a swimming pool on top of it. He even went so far as to have an Olympic diving champion come and dive into the pool during the day. Bill also invited Walter Hagen, five-time PGA Champion, to be the Grand Marshal of the event. Hagen, who was in his late 60s, didn't show up until we got to about the eighth tee. He drove up in a big limousine, got out dressed in his finest, and said to Hogan and Snead, "I didn't want to take any of the glory away from you young guys at the start."
>
> That night after the match there was Ben Hogan, Walter, a sports writer and me sitting together having a drink. They got talking and Ben brought up the time he received a call from Hagen. "You know when the phone

rang at one o'clock in the morning and Valerie came back and said, 'It's Walter Hagen,' I figured I'd better answer it. Walter, if you hadn't made that call that night, I would never have played in the British Open. But you said to me, *'Ben you owe it to your country to go over there and win the tournament.'*"

And that is why Hogan went to Carnoustie that year and became the Open Champion.

Ben Hogan was glad he got the call.

Surprise!

Mr. Fred Beck tells us a few years back about the fun-loving pro shop staff at Sun Valley in Idaho run by head pro Joe Moeller. "From the golf-shop door, a path leads to the first tee. The path crosses a little brook by means of a rustic bridge. While crossing the bridge, newcomers to the course are likely to see a beautiful new golf ball down in the babbling brook, under six inches of water. About 20 people a day find that ball. Some try to fish it out with a golf club. Others roll up their sleeves and reach for it. But that ball is firmly (but secretly) bolted to a rock. It is fun to watch the uninitiated fall for the anchored-ball trick because nearly always the victim is the first to laugh."

He "Barely" Had Time to Putt

If you want to meet one of the most gregarious pros in Ohio, go to Youngstown Country Club and look up George Bellino. He is a muscular package of Italian fun with a golf swing that has more loops than a roller coaster…but he can play. As a youngster he worked with a crazy bunch of guys on the golf course. One of them was named Flanagan, but everyone called him "Cater." Now Cater didn't get dealt a full deck of cards, so his behavior was, trying to say it politely, unpredictable. After work he was out playing skins with these guys and they were on the seventh hole. Right alongside number seven a man had a swimming pool at his house. It was a real hot day, about 90 degrees, and Cater's group was waiting for the players to leave the seventh green. Suddenly Cater took off all of his clothes and jumped into this man's pool. Then, with no clothes on, he came back and hit a shot to the green.

As his group got on the green a car pulled up and in it was the man who owned the pool. He had driven down the road that borders the seventh fairway. Seeing Cater on the green, he pulled out a gun and said, "You know what? I'm going to shoot you. You jumped into that pool with my kids and you had no clothes on!"

Cater, who again was a little different, got over his ball and said, "Wait till I finish my putt."

THE GREAT SHOTGUN START

If you ever run into Lee Trevino, ask him what was the single most important assist he ever got in his career to help propel him to stardom. I will wager that his answer will be it was when Bill Eschenbrener, golf director at the El Paso Country Club in Texas, went to bat for him to get his membership into the PGA of America. Bill, a respected teacher, player, and administrator in golf offered to turn in his own membership if they wouldn't accept Lee. They finally did, which allowed Trevino a chance to qualify for PGA Tour events. He qualified for his first tournament and then made something like 12 straight cuts, which automatically placed him in the following week's events. This run put him on the exempt money list for the next year. In that next year he won the U.S. Open. The rest is history.

But not everything that Bill Eschenbrener did in his career went exactly to plan. Take for instance his great shotgun start. Here is how he told it to me:

> I had this bright idea that I wanted to make our shotgun starts more effective. We'd had this July 4th celebration, and to start off the fireworks we sent up these salute bombs. When they go up they make a huge BOOM, exploding with a vengeance. I thought that would make a

hell of an impressive shotgun start at one of our golf events. So I tried it during a member/guest event and it went over great. Everyone thought it was terrific. To shoot it off, we placed the bomb in a six-inch steel cylinder that had a plate on the bottom and was buried about three feet in the ground near the shop. The bomb would then come shooting out of there like a rocket to great heights before exploding.

The male members liked it so much that I decided to do it for my ladies' member/guest as well. The wind was blowing about 40 miles an hour that day, as it can in West Texas. I had the salute bomb fuse just sticking above the ground. I kept lighting my matches and lighting my matches, but the gusting wind kept blowing them out. I got down to my last match. I bent over close to the launch cylinder hole with the match and cupped my hand around it. What I didn't know was that it had already lit on the one before. The rocket ignited with me bent down there and flew out right next to my face. It knocked me back onto the ground and I was stunned. I'm lucky it didn't kill me. I finally got up and walked into the shop. The staff was completely unaware as to what had just happened. They looked at me kind of funny but I didn't know why, so I walked into the restroom and looked into the mirror. My left eyebrow was white, as was the hair on the left side of my head. I wiped my face and the hair and eyebrow all came off. I later had to go to the presentation and give the prizes for the ladies luncheon with no eyebrow or hair on my left side. In spite of my mishap, everybody seemed to love the new shotgun start so we decided to keep the thing going.

The next year in time for the men's member/guest I had a nice new thousand-dollar scoreboard built. It was located about 30 feet from the launch site. We got the bombs for the event but I wasn't aware that they were four-inch rather than the six-inch size. My new assistant was to do the lighting; I had decided after the last experience to retire from launch duty. By now, we had learned to ignite them with a cigarette attached to the end of an old golf shaft. This being his first time and not knowing the difference, he mistakenly put a four-inch bomb into a six-inch pipe. Poof! The rocket took off but traveled only about 50 feet in the air. It came down and landed right on the roof of the scoreboard and blew up. Shingles and score sheets flew everywhere. That one was costly. Still the members liked the idea. I guess it was just more exciting; I certainly could vouch for that.

So the time came around again for the ladies' member/guest where the year before I had my hair loss experience. We were in the midst of building a new pro shop. With the expansion we had to take our launch pipe out of the ground. I told my assistant to go over to the maintenance area and set the launch pipe on the ground since it had a flat steel bottom, and maybe pack some sand around it for support. I instructed him to then put the bomb in, light it, and run like hell. What happened was when he lit it he got so excited that he accidentally pulled it back toward him. He luckily dove to the ground, evidenced by the fact that his arms were all scratched up when he came back to the shop. He told me the rocket flew right over his head toward the 12th tee where some of the players were. *My gosh*, I thought, *we'd better get out there*, so we hopped into a cart and headed toward 12. The ladies were in the fairway. We discovered the errant bomb had blown up about 30 feet above their heads when they were on the tee and they almost peed their panties. They were not happy! And that was the end of the great shotgun starts.

The Man Knew How to Order

Before leaving our thoughts of El Paso Country Club, I once visited there as a representative of the PGA of America to make a presentation at a Pro-President golf event. The schedule was to include lunch, 18 holes, cocktails, then the dinner at which I was to speak. I arrived at the clubhouse just in time for the lunch and saw a long table where several professionals were sitting with their club presidents. I didn't know many pros in that section so I chose to sit next to a man on the end who was most certainly a president as he was still dressed in a business suit.

After we introduced one another, a waitress came over with a menu to let us make our selections for lunch. When she offered a menu to the president next to me he said, "I don't need that." He repeated that statement when she offered it again.

He was not a member there so the waitress was a bit confused. She said, "What do you mean, sir?"

He said, "I don't need a menu. Just give me whatever the assistant pros eat, because they always eat better than anybody in the club."

It Still Was a Secret

Few professionals have served their club as faithfully and have been as well liked as Ken Weiler was at Park Ridge in Chicago. He tells this story about Skip Alexander, a two-time winner on the PGA Tour, Ryder Cup member, and a former North-South Amateur champion:

> During the late 1940s and early '50s Alexander was one of the 10 best players in the country and played a lot of golf with Ben Hogan. My family and I were visiting him in St. Petersburg, Florida, during one Christmas holi-

day and my son asked him, "You've played often with Ben Hogan, what is Hogan's secret?"

Skip, who spent enough time in the Carolinas to have a southern accent, said, "Let me tell you a story."

"We were playing in Memphis and it was after the second round. I had finished and wanted to practice but they didn't have a good practice facility at the club where we played. So I went over to the Memphis Country Club to hit balls later that afternoon. I was by myself on the practice tee hitting balls, and here comes Ben Hogan down the hill with a chair in his hand. He sets it up right behind me and sits there. I hit three or four balls and Hogan looks and looks and finally says, 'That's it, that's it!' Then I hit four or five more balls and Hogan again says, 'That's it, that's it!'

"So I finally turned to Ben and I said, 'Ben, what does, 'that's it' mean?' And Ben picked up his chair and walked back up the hill. And that's what I know a-bout Ben Hogan's se-cret."

Hogan kept the meaning of "that's it" to himself.

It's More Humorous When You Are Watching

Fred Griffin, Top 100 Teacher at Grand Cypress G.C., tells of playing in a tournament in San Antonio, Texas.

It was about 32 degrees out, pretty cold for golf. The friend I was playing with was not having a good day at all. On the 17th hole he hooked his drive across a small body of water into the opposite fairway. It must have been 70 yards off line. There was a cast-iron pipe that stretched across the water to another fairway. It was a long ride around the water so he stopped his cart adjacent to the pipe and to where his ball was across the water. He had decided he was going to walk across that pipe to his ball. He took his clubs from the cart and started across. About halfway, his spikes started slipping and he fell right into the water—clubs, bag, shoes, everything. He was so embarrassed that he just stood up and walked the rest of the way across the water with his bag above his head like a guy carrying his army rifle while walking through a swamp. He hit his shot, and then to our disbelief he waded back across through the water with his bag again held high in the air. He got into his cart, drove to the green, chipped his ball on, and while walking across the green prepared to putt, his feet squishing with each step. It was so cold; he had to be freezing, but that didn't stop us from busting out laughing. Unfortunately, he didn't catch the humor.

THE AUTOMATIC "GIMME"

The year was 1968. The new pro in town was Mark Darnell and he had just been invited to play golf. The town was Augusta, Georgia; the course where the match was to be played...Augusta National. Mark had been on the PGA Tour for a bit and served as both an assistant and head pro before coming to Augusta. He then took over the reigns at the West Lake Country Club, which he continued to direct for 34 years. His host at "The National" was none other than the irascible majordomo, Cliff Roberts. Roberts was a high single-digit handicap player, and the game was a better ball of two for $20. On the first hole Roberts rolled a putt up about three or four feet from the hole and promptly raked it in, a personal gimme. On the next hole after an iron shot missed the green, Roberts chipped it up to about three to four feet then repeated the previous "gimme" procedure. This type of behavior continued for another couple of holes until

Cliff Roberts ruled this place

Roberts went over to rake another of his putts away when Darnell put his putter across the line so that Roberts couldn't reach the ball and said, "Mr. Roberts, we are playing for $20."

Roberts looked directly at Darnell and said, "Mark, I run this club."

Darnell withdrew his putter and said, "That's good Mr. Roberts."

AN ACUTE SENSE OF HEARING

Joe Magarace was the teaching professional at the Old South Country Club in Lothian, Maryland, which is directly under the flight path for Andrews Air Base. This is his story. Tom Clancy, the famous author of *Hunt For Red October, Patriot Games, Executive Orders,* and other military-based novels, contacted Joe. Clancy wanted a playing lesson, which they scheduled to be held in three weeks. Once the two of them were on the course, Magarace was amazed at Clancy's ability to identify, simply by sound, the aircraft that were regularly flying overhead. Without looking up Clancy would say, "That's a V22 Osprey," or an "AC 119 Shadow," or "C 141 Starlifter." Between plane identification pauses, the lesson apparently went very well since Clancy requested another playing lesson in three more weeks.

As the time for the second lesson approached, Magarace looked at the starting sheet and noticed that a member had taken the spot immediately behind them. Joe made a note to tell the member he could certainly play through if the lesson was going too slowly.

When the day of the lesson arrived, the member showed up early. Because of a superstitious quirk, he requested the counter staff to assemble for him an entire dozen Titleist DTs all with red number 3s. To do that the staff had to open three additional boxes of a dozen to accommodate the member, but they did.

Clancy and Magarace played quickly enough that the member following did not need to play through. But while they were on the seventh fairway preparing to hit a shot, they heard a loud shout of "FORE!" coming from the sixth tee where the member was teeing off. Magarace turned away, and while doing so told Clancy to "Look out, here comes a Titlest DT Red #3, and they can be deadly."

A second later the ball landed at Clancy's feet. When he looked down to identify it he exclaimed, "Hey, it *is* a Titleist DT Red #3! How did you know that?"

Joe simply said, "I heard it coming."

In Magarace's own words, "Because I did not give Tom enough information, to this day I think he believes I really have the ability to differentiate golf balls in flight by their sound."

On Second Thought

There are some people who specialize in a singular aspect of their profession, thus becoming recognized experts in what they do. There are others who are generalists and can do a lot of things well but aren't experts. Then there are a few who specialize in doing many things all expertly well. MacGregor "Mac" Hunter is one of them. Here is his lineup of accomplishments: head PGA professional at Riviera C. C. in Los Angeles for 22 years; Golf Director at Princeville in Hawaii; California Amateur Champion; quarter finalist in the U.S. Amateur; owner and principal designer of the Auld Classic Golf Company; golf course architect, having designed 14 of his own and five redesigns; tournament organizer; and teaching expert.

When Mac was at Riviera he had a member named General Moncado about whom he tells this anecdote:

While it may not have been a household name, Moncado

formerly was a five-star general in the Philippines, and a four-star general for the United States. He was president of the Philippine Federation of America. That particular organization had to pay him a dollar a person for every Filipino who worked in the lettuce fields in Salinas, California.

The general was a big promoter of golf. He backed Lloyd Mangrum, "Porky" Oliver, "Dutch" Harrison, in other words, some of the best players of their day. We used to fly up to his lettuce fields in Salinas and play a tournament where he'd put up $10,000 of his own money, which wasn't a small amount in those days. The general used to play a lot at the old Fox Hills club that has since been plowed under. Some of the games were with Joe Louis, "Babe" Didrickson, "Smiley" Quick; but he gave up on them because they hustled him. He liked to play at Riviera so he would call me and say, "Mac, I am going to pay my way. Would you like to play with me today?"

I would say, "I would be delighted, General."

He would offer, "I pay you $1,000," which was big money for a playing lesson. Then he would come out and we would have our game.

On one occasion the general did play in the U.S. Amateur and shot a 72 in the morning qualifying round. They put a scorer out with him in the afternoon round and he shot a 92. So he did have a way of massaging his scores. Usually he would hire two or three caddies, one of which would get out in front of him, like a forecaddie, to mark his drive. That caddy would find his ball, clean it, put it down in a better spot, and the general would arrive and play his next shot. If the shot from the fairway wasn't on the green somewhere, the caddy would pick it up and put it there. That was the way he played. In the meantime he would carry on a conversation with you. So you'd talk and you'd play.

This one particular day at Riviera the general had come out for a game, but I didn't play with him. "Buddy" Holscher, one of California's outstanding players, did. The word came in that the general was setting the course record. He came into the golf shop where I was at the counter. He said, "Mac, Mac, I shot 63 today."

I said, "That's wonderful general. The course record here is 66 and I have it."

"Oh Mac, today I shot 67."

I said, "That's very good general. Congratulations!"

A Quick Exit

Here's another story from MacGregor:

We played the Beverly Hills Open in Los Angeles at the old California Country Club, which has since given way to development. It was right next to Twentieth Century Fox and was a big-time gamblers' den. This was in the early 1950s and most of the best players of the day were there.

Ray Mangrum was leading the tournament. He was the brother to U.S. Open and Masters champion Lloyd Mangrum, and was one hell of a player. A lot of people say he was better than his brother. Ray had just finished the ninth hole and had a one-shot lead with nine holes left to play. The 10th was a par-3, about 130 yards, maybe a little 8-iron in those days. He loved to gamble, and it so happened that that particular day they had a high stakes poker game going in the "snake pit" underneath the clubhouse deck that overlooked the 10th hole. Mangrum hit his tee shot on the 10th about 15 feet from the hole. Just after he hit, a guy stuck his head out of the window and yelled, "We have a game on, table stakes, $1,000 a head," which at that time probably meant a $6,000 to $10,000 a hand game. Mangrum picked up his putt, walked straight to the "den," and they never saw him again on that day. That was it—the leader of the Beverly Hills Open. That's heavy duty, but it's the God's truth. He walked right off the green and headed for the den.

THE LAST THANK YOU

John Gerring is not only a Top 100 Teacher by *Golf Magazine* standards, but he is also a Top 100 person in my book. I would call him a "throwback pro." No, it doesn't mean if you have him you want to throw him back (although that's what John would say). It means his style harkens back to a time when the golf professional was the epitome of a gentleman, dedicated strongly to the service of the member, conservative in thought and action, loyal, hardworking, a tough taskmaster; though he may not be your best buddy, he would be your best friend if you were in need.

While serving the Atlanta Country Club, John initiated a program with his staff that whenever dealing with a member, the staff person was to always, always, always say the last "thank you." On ladies' day a member (we'll call her Mrs. Stewart) came into the shop just before her tee time carrying a fairway wood that needed some minor repair. The string whipping around the hosel had come loose and needed to be rewound and tied off. John took the club and told her that it would be ready for her at the turn when she came through.

After the front nine Mrs. Stewart came back into the shop and John handed her the club. She asked the charge for the service and John said, "No charge, we are happy to do it."

She responded with a "thank you."

To which John countered, "No, thank you, Mrs. Stewart, we enjoy serving you."

Now it appears that Mrs. Stewart was aware of John's last "thank you" program because she then said as she approached the door, "I appreciate that, John. But that was a kind thing you did for me so I want to thank you."

John again cleverly countered with a "Thank you for saying that, Mrs. Stewart."

Upon which Mrs. Stewart walked out the door, then poked her head back inside just long enough to say, "Thank you John!" and fled.

When Mrs. Stewart finished her round she came by the pro shop, and was amused by what she saw. A large paper banner was posted in the pro shop window. It read, "THANK YOU, MRS. STEWART!"

Three days later there was a phone call at the shop for John. He answered and a woman's voice said, "John, check the *Atlanta Constitution* personals for today." He did and found a short message. *John, Thank You. Mrs. Stewart.* It was one time he didn't get the last thank you.

He Just Liked the Place

I never met anybody who didn't like PGA professional John Haines, whose most profane utterance is "Good Golly Miss Molly." That usually comes when he hits a bad shot, which isn't very often. While serving as the director of golf at Teton Pines in Jackson Hole, Wyoming, he recalled one of the several times that he had an opportunity to play with President Clinton:

> The first time I played with President Clinton I was a little intimidated. One reason was that we had 14 golf carts following us, Secret Service, etc., which was a bit unnerving. There was a group of members up in front and I thought, *Boy I hope those members don't hold us up.* We also had a group of members behind. When we got to the sixth tee I asked the President, "Mr. President, how do you like Jackson Hole?" Well, I shouldn't have done that. He went on and on talking about Jackson Hole. By the time he got done answering that one question, the group that was in front of us on the sixth fairway when we started had now hit their second shots to the seventh green. I had to say to him, "Mr. President, we'd better get going. I think we're holding up the golf course." But he sure liked the place!

Now We Know What "Fore!" Means

You always looked up to a guy like Jake Wursckul. For one reason he was 6 feet, 5 inches tall, and another, he was a respected pro in the state of Washington. Jake had just finished a beginning series of lessons with two women who had done quite well under his tutelage. It was now time to take their game to the course, which they did on a Friday afternoon at the club. That weekend there was a large party for the members at the club-house with Jake in attendance. While he was standing alone, his two recently-initiated students came over, looked up, and said, "We are so embarrassed."

"Why?" asked Jake, "What did you do?"

"Well, we played yesterday."

"Oh, don't let that bother you," Jake said, "The first time out the scores are always high."

"No, it's not that," they replied. "We actually hit the ball pretty well. It's what we did."

"Okay, what did you do?"

"Well, you know when you took us out on the course on the last lesson to show us the different tees for men and women, how to get from the green to the tee, where to set the flagstick, and all of that?"

"Yes," Jake said, "I remember."

"Well while we were out there someone shouted 'FORE' but we didn't understand because you didn't say anything about it."

"And?"

"Well we didn't know, so when we played and hit our shots we shouted, 'ONE,' then, 'TWO,' 'THREE,' 'FOUR,' 'FIVE,' 'SIX,' and 'SEVEN' out loud after each shot until we made it into the cup. After three holes a man came over and asked, 'What are you ladies doing?' *That's when we found out what FORE means.*"

What a Memory

PGA professional Tom Jewell once asked Sam Snead what it was like to play with Hogan. Snead said, "Few words were ex-changed. On the first tee, Ben would say, 'Good luck,' and some-times 'nice round' on the 18th green." Sam also revealed that he didn't like Hogan's swing, too flat. So he would watch Ben ad-dress the ball, and as Hogan began his backswing, Snead would turn his head and follow Hogan's ball in flight. But he wouldn't watch the swing.

Tom also remembered playing in a Pro-Am with Kathy Whitworth, Sam Snead and two amateurs at Bardmoor C.C. in Largo, Florida, and told this about the day:

> It was a thrill to play with Sam and Kathy. I wanted to watch Sam's swing up close and listen to his stories. I had heard that he remembered every golf shot he ever made. I told him I learned to play golf by caddying at the Oak Hill Country Club in Rochester, New York, under Charlie McKenna, the head professional. Hearing Oak Hill, Sam described almost every hole on the East course.
>
> On the sixth hole at Bardmoor a spectator approached Sam and said, "Sam, I saw you make one of your greatest shots."
>
> Sam said, "Where was that?"
>
> The fan said, "New Orleans, Louisiana."
>
> Sam said, "Lakewood Country Club."
>
> The fan said, "Yes."
>
> Sam said, "1968."
>
> The fan said, "Yes."
>
> Sam said, "Sixth hole—behind a big tree—right of the fairway."
>
> The fan said, "Yes."
>
> Sam said, "I was 207 yards to the flag—I hit a cut 3-iron around the tree to three feet from the hole."
>
> The fan said, "That's unbelievable, Sam—that's exactly what happened."
>
> Sam said, "Yeah, and I missed the damned putt."

Forgot Something?

Jack Tindale, PGA professional from Rochester, N.Y., is into the mechanics and theory of putting in a big way but tells a story that has nothing to do with the short stroke:

> There is a club just outside of Rochester called Green Hills. It's owned by members, mostly of Italian descent, who got together and bought the club. Every Saturday morning this group has an automatic tee time. It starts at eight a.m. and goes through till nine. There are all kinds of bets and presses and everything you can image among this animated group. *They like action.*
>
> A few years ago the whole gang was around the first tee on Saturday, as usual, making bets and teeing off. Louie, one of the big promoters of the game, was late. When his car pulled into the parking lot everybody started yelling and screaming, "Louie, get over here." So Louie jumped out of his car, golf shoes in hand, and headed for the tee, signaling for an attendant to get his clubs and put them on a cart.
>
> He walked up on the tee and started tying his shoes, making games as his group was teeing off. "I'll play you 5-5 and 5, and you, and you the same. You get two shots and you four." With the bets all settled, he jumped in his cart and his group headed down the fairway.
>
> There was a delay on the tee. The professional, Joe Diego, came out of the golf shop and said, "What the heck is the holdup?"
>
> The players on the tee told Joe it looked like Louie's group lost a ball. So Joe jumped in a cart and drove down the fairway to find out what was going on. "What's the matter?" he asked the foursome.

"We can't find Louie's ball," was the response from one of the players.

Joe asked, "What kind of ball were you playing, Louie?'"

Louie said, "I don't remember."

"What do you mean you don't remember?"

Louie said, "I don't think I hit one off the first tee." And he hadn't. He got so much into his bets he forgot to tee it up.

MEET IVAN GANTZ

Speaking of characters, how I wish I could introduce you to Ivan Gantz, now long departed from Earth's fairways. He had such beautiful blue eyes that sparkled with mischief. He was a warm human being who cared about people and would spend time just listening to them. However, on a golf course he was known for his volcanic temper. Here are some Ivan stories.

In Dan Jenkins' book, *The Dogged Victims of Inexorable Fate,* Don January said, "The first time I ever saw Ivan he was walking down a fairway parallel to mine....Blood was streaming down his forehead over his nose. The man had hit himself in the head with his putter because he'd blown a short one." He'd heard of Ivan diving into creeks, banging his head with a stone, and rolling and tossing in the grass. Another writer, Charles Price, claimed Ivan even threw clubs on the driving range.

A pro friend of mine said he had heard all the Ivan stories so the first time he played with Ivan he was watching for some eruption, particularly after Ivan three-putted 18. Nothing happened...he thought. Until he looked around for Ivan to sign the scorecard and saw Ivan sticking his hands in a crown-of-thorns bush for punishment after another three putt.

Putting was his nemesis. He once three-putted a green, walked over to the fringe while holding his putter against his chest, fell backward into the bunker and started scooping sand on himself saying, "I'm going to bury myself alive."

Gene Borek, PGA professional from the Metropolis Club in New York and onetime second day leader of the U.S. Open, tells of playing in a Tour qualifying event with Ivan at the Mayfair Golf Club in Sanford, Florida. In those days qualifying tournaments were pretty casual. You showed up, paid your money, shot your score, and you either were in or out. Ivan occasionally liked to have his dog along with him when he played and brought him along on this day. Gene didn't care much, but the other player in the group was getting irritated by Ivan's dog running around while he was trying to focus. After several holes with Ivan's dog running back and forth around the green then through a bunker, the player said, "Ivan, will you please mark your dog?"

Ivan's eyesight began to fail as he aged. While playing in a small event his ball reached one of the greens but was still a long way away from the cup. The caddy had removed the flagstick and was holding it vertically some 10 feet to the right of the cup. Ivan lined up for the flagstick and hit it quickly before anyone realized where he was aiming. There was an old cup just short of where the flagstick was being held. Ivan's ball rolled right over it with a little bounce. "What the heck is going on!" he shouted. "Is there a lid on that hole?" Then as he walked up and realized his mistake, he looked at the old cup, smiled, and said, "I guess there is."

A Lesson Incognito

Johnny Myers has been a mainstay professional in the Gulf states for many years teaching, playing, and writing. In his words he tells this story:

I wrote this article called "Spring for Power" for a national golf magazine. The idea was to lower your head and drive your legs through, and you come up with increased power. I had a gentleman call me from Florida and he said, "Johnny, I want to come over to Louisiana and work on this spring for power." I told him that was fine, so we set up a time.

He came, and we went straight to the range. The man was about six foot five and weighed about 120 pounds. I've never seen anybody—including John Daly—who had such a long backswing. He raised the club and turned so far, bending his left arm, that the clubhead pointed to the ground. His first statement was, "What about this spring for power?"

Well, I can't teach a man to spring when he has the club wrapped around his neck, so I said, "Did anybody ever mention your left arm?"

He said, "No, nobody."

Luckily I had a graph-check camera with me. I said, "Do you mind if I take a shot and let you see it?"

When he saw the picture he said, "Man, I didn't realize my backswing was that long and my left arm was so bent." Well, we didn't get too much into "springing for power," which is what he came for.

Three years later I was teaching at this club in Chicago. They called the range and said, "Johnny, I'm sending a lesson down to you." A couple of minutes later I looked up and here is this same tall, thin man, coming down to take a lesson. I couldn't believe it! I thought, *Good God, here's a man who came to me three years ago and I didn't help him with what he wanted. I go to a big city with millions of people, and here I get him again.*

So I pulled my cap way down low and didn't look up. Of all the lessons I've ever given, it's the only one where I never looked any higher than the player's waist. He didn't know I was in Chicago, and I tried to make sure he never found out.

READY FOR WHAT?

John Allen spent 11 years chasing a playing career on the PGA Tour before he chose to go in another direction. He recalls playing in the tournament that was then known simply as "The Crosby" at Pebble Beach. He told about his warm-up period prior to his round, and his story went like this:

> In those days the caddies stood out on the range. We hit our balls toward them while they picked them up. The mark of a good player was that his caddy didn't have to move much. I was the first one there until Jack Nicklaus came to hit beside me. Then Arnold Palmer came to hit on the other side of me. I got so nervous that I hit one 40 yards right and my caddy went running after it. Then I hit one 40 yards left so he now had to run 80 yards to get it. I was so flustered that I whistled for him to come in, yelling, "Let's go, I'm ready."
>
> Jack looked out at my breathless caddy, turned to me and said, *"Ready for what?"*

John also remembers his first tournament on the Tour when he was paired with Chi Chi Rodriquez. As he tells it:

> It was the second hole, and I had honors since I had birdied the first. I hit a great shot close to the pin on the par-3. Suddenly a huge Great Dane came bounding

Here Gary Player is between Arnie and Jack where John Allen was once.

across the fairway, through the bunker, onto the green, grabbed my ball and took off running. Quick as a whip and perfectly straight-faced, Chi Chi said, "Don't let him run out of bounds with your ball." I took off after that dog for all I was worth. After about 50 yards I remembered the rule that it doesn't matter where the outside agency (the dog in the case) goes with your ball, you get to place it as near as possible to where it was picked up. I turned to see Chi Chi and the rest of the foursome roaring in laughter at the rookie.

What Do You Suppose Were His Answers?

Every Wednesday morning for 30 years on ladies' day at his club, a fellow golf professional had been giving brief rules sessions along with a golf tip. He sent me a list of his favorite rules questions throughout those years. They are:

"Excuse me Mr. Professional, but could you tell me...?"

1. If the ball falls off the tee in the fairway, are you allowed to re-tee it?
2. If your mulligan is not used on the front nine, can you use it on the back?
3. Is the penalty for a whiff stroke and distance?
4. Are you allowed to play a lost ball?
5. Are summer rules in effect when the temperature goes below 40 degrees?
6. Can you ask a fellow competitor your score if you've lost count?
7. Does the 19th hole have to be played in sequence?

And my favorite...

8. What happens if you swing at the ball, miss it, and then find out it is not yours?

Do you know the answers? Actually, #8 really needs your attention. The answer is: in four-ball competition, if you swing at a ball that is not yours and miss it, you incur a two-stroke penalty for playing the wrong ball; in match play it is a loss of hole.

Some of the questions asked here are not in the book.

THE PGA'S POET LAUREATE

While he may not be officially designated as such, in my mind "Stoney" Brown of Boise, Idaho, is the PGA's Poet Laureate. To my knowledge, no PGA professional has ever created as much original poetry as Stoney. He has entertained his members and guests of the Crane Creek Country Club by writing clever verse to commemorate events that are played at his facility. They have been privately published in a soft cover book appropriately titled, *A Collection of Golf Poetry and Short Stories, Written by an Idaho Club Professional*. Here are a couple of my favorites.

Ladies' Club Championship 1989... "The Expert"

Right up to the shop pulled a late-model car,
    and slowing it came to a stop
It had vanity plates with the message of "PAR"
    and an Augusta green Naugahyde top.
Then out from the car, from the driver's side door
    came a woman much darkened by sun.
She knew the score from the look that she wore
    and she headed for tee number one.

She moved with the ease and the grace of a pro
    and envy filled all those she passed.
Her shoes cost a couple of hundred or so
    and her bag was of leather, to last!

Her custom-made clubs had a glint and sheen
    and she shouldered them well in her stride.
Her outfit was fuchsia with stripes of lime-green,
    her demeanor denoted great pride.

It was quiet for sure, when she stepped to the tee
    and she pulled on her glove with great care.
When she teed up her ball, many eyes strained to see
    and her target she fixed with a stare.

With a slight forward press, from her perfect address,
    she turned until ready to spring
And so braced for the test, fully coiled more-or-less
    all awaited the rest of her swing.

And the club started down with a twist of her hips
    and a tug as she gave it the gas—
But some grins quickly formed on her gallery's lips
    when she whiffed it and fell on her ass!

Ladies' Tri-Club 1986... "Looking Good"

Now here's a suggestion for improving our game,
    a thought that's at least worth a penny.
We'll reverse that old saw that has garnered such fame,
    you know—"It's not how, but how many."
We'll dump the "how many" and focus on "how,"
    giving points just for style and for dress.
When it's "how" that's important, it might allow
    more golfers the chance to impress.

We could forgo the range and the blisters and such,
    to shop for the latest in clothes.
Learn some finish positions to use in a clutch.
    When you shank—it's important to pose!

We'd give credit for properly leaning on putters
    and points for the odd, icy stare.

Those with nonchalance and the great fairway strutters
    should rack up some points here and there.

As scores are replaced with criterion expressive,
    ball striking won't even matter.
The winners will be those with styles most impressive—
    or those with a good line of chatter.

The game could be different in one other way.
    Dump the ball. Now that's a good rule!
We could stare, style and strut for the entire day,
    And all we could lose is our cool!

Though some will not like what this prose might convey,
    Remember the last score you took.
And don't be a shnnook, for it's not how you play—
    but it DAMN SURE is how you look!

"Thank you, Stoney."

OBSERVATIONS AND QUIPS

North Carolina has turned out some fine golf professionals. One of the best was "Buck" Adams. He once described Miller Barber's unorthodox golf swing in the following manner. "It looks like one of those taffy-making machines at the carnival, going six different directions but coming out all right in the end."

———————

Eddie Famula, "The Fam" to his fellow pros, was an outstanding player from the New Jersey Section of the PGA. Eddie is a small, quiet, unassuming guy who still manages to have a clever sense of humor as depicted by this observation of his. "I was at this one club for eight years and figure I may be the only pro in the history of the PGA who satisfied their members 100%. Yep, that's right, 100%. Thirty percent when I came and seventy percent when I left."

_____

The greatest PGA professional to ever come out of Tullahoma, Tennessee has to be "Hubbie" Smith, serving in his last position as Director of Golf at The Concord. He once made the following observation in his best Tennessee accent: "Hell, golf's easy. All ya' gotta' do is TEE IT, HIT IT, HUNT IT, HOLE IT, AND RECORD IT!"

_____

Short game and bunker expert Paul Runyan, when playing a shot to a green that he couldn't hold with his fairway wood, noted that many bunkers surrounded it. He asked his playing partner Jimmy Demaret, "Which one of those bunkers is smoothest?"

QUOTES

"Golf is easy, because no amount of stupidity can keep you from finishing the 18 holes." **Greg McHatton**, PGA professional

"The only difference between a New York City policeman and a private club golf professional is that the policeman knows who's got a gun at his head and ready to pull the trigger." **Tom Shea,** PGA professional

"Life's ultimate mulligan." **Dave Marr** (describing the Senior Tour, now Champions Tour)

"You ask me why they call the long grass on the course rough? Because, that's what it is, rough! Otherwise they would call it 'easy.'" **Hubert Green**

Golf Brings a Special Message

Most of the writing in this book has a light or humorous bent.
But Chapter Five, "Golf Brings a Special Message," is different.
It presents stories that offer more than a punch-line.

THE MOST SINCERE ADVICE

George Knudson was one of Canada's greatest golfers, a former PGA Tour player of 14 years who once was given the accolade by Jack Nicklaus as "having the best swing out there." George definitely did have a wonderfully disciplined and efficient swing that brought him 12 victories south of the Canadian border. There were two habits in his life, however, which were less disciplined: drinking and smoking. The drinking caused his skills to deteriorate prematurely and resulted in his leaving the Tour too early. George settled back in Toronto where he began to study the golf swing from a teacher's standpoint. Many golfers quickly sought him out for lessons, knowing of his great experience and talent. Teaching soon became the focus in his professional life. By this time he had overcome the alcohol addiction but not the cigarettes.

At the age of 51 George Knudson was lying in a Toronto hospital dying of lung cancer. This was just at the time when a new book he had been working on entitled *Natural Golf* had come off the presses. A very close friend of George's was Ben Kern, then golf director at The National in Toronto. Once George entered the hospital, Ben visited him regularly. On one of those visits during the last two weeks of George's life, Ben brought in a copy of *Natural Golf.* At the end of their visit together Ben asked George if he would sign the book and write something in it that might be helpful to Ben's students. George indicated he was too tired at the moment but he'd have it ready for Ben on their next meeting. That occurred two days later. After talking with one another, Ben was getting up to leave when George said, "Here's your book. I signed it." Ben got out in the hall and anxiously opened up the cover of the book. This is what it said, "Ben, Tell your students two things. 1. *It is difficult in life to do something if you don't understand what you are trying to do.* Ben, tell your students, 2. *Change is not easy. George*

The Toy Department

Back in the 1920s when Herb Graffis, co-founder of *Golfdom Magazine,* was just a cub reporter for the *Chicago Herald-Tribune,* he took his lunch break at a bar where you could get a free snack with your beer. While sitting at the bar he recognized one of the renowned news editorial writers enter and come toward him. "Hey kid," he said, sitting down next to Herb, "I've seen you around the paper, what do you do?"

Graffis responded proudly, "I write sports, sir."

"Oh, the toy department," replied the columnist.

Herb felt demeaned. Yet as he later thought more about it, he acknowledged that the veteran scribe had a point. Herb thought about the fact that when a person goes to a department store (in those days the "biggies" were multistoried with each floor specializing in some category) the most fun floor, particularly at Christmas, was the one that featured the toy department. That is how Herb always felt that golf should present itself. He told professionals that their occupation was in the "toy department of life" and they were the floor managers.

A HUGE REGRET

I supposed we all have things that have happened in our lives that we would change if we could. In my golf career one stands out in particular. I think about it often.

My wife, four children, and I were living in Oregon. Because of my academic status having earned a Ph.D., the PGA had asked me to be a reviewer of the manuscripts for the new classification of Master Professional. At that time there were fewer than 10 Masters who had qualified. One of the requirements was to write a Master's thesis on some part of the golf business and this hurdle put off a good many candidates, as it was very time-consuming. An additional barrier for some was that it was not a familiar part of their accustomed work. I had gone through the rigors of thesis-writing both for my Master's and Doctorate and was familiar with many of the conditions of style that the PGA was asking to be met. That included footnoting, bibliography, grammar, punctuation, as well as form and content.

The PGA forwarded to me a manuscript from a famous professional, Mr. Joe Novak, former president of the PGA, head professional at the Bel Aire Country Club in Los Angeles, author of instruction books, and teacher of note. He had pretty much done everything that you could in the golf business. By his record he was a demonstrated master of the profession.

From a content standpoint Mr. Novak's thesis was acceptable. He wrote on his favorite subject, teaching, and he certainly knew the material. But he had failed to follow the guidelines for some of the form requirements, therefore not exactly meeting the criteria. I identified those failures in red pencil and sent the thesis back with a letter saying that when these minor things were cleaned up and the corrections made he could resubmit it for approval. He never did. It never came back. He must have been embarrassed that it didn't pass the first time. And for what reason did it fail? Technicalities! It had nothing to do with how well he had served the members at Bel Aire, what contributions he had made to his profession and the PGA, nor his help in promoting the game. It was about trivia. Over a hundred other professionals became Masters after his attempt, including myself. Yet few of us could live up to the title as well as he would have. Joe Novak was truly a "Master Professional," and I am so sorry, Joe, that you were never accorded that recognition.

THE POWER OF GOLF

In reminding my fellow golf professionals of the power of the game in which they are involved, I created the following example: What other game would entice people to:

1. Be attracted enough to go to a driving range on a cold March night in the North to hit lumpy range balls off rubber mats?

2. Show up on the course at 6 a.m. to stroke "rooster tail" putts, drag pants legs through the wet grass, and trace zigzag patterns of frustration from one rough to another?

Yes, golf is easy to fall in love with.

3. Play in snow, desert heat, rain, and even life-threatening lightning, when they don't have to?

4. Get six-figure executives to give up one week of their vacation to park cars at a golf tournament and think they are having fun, even though they are ferrying mostly officials and media types?

5. Remain as the solitary figure on the range after the sun has disappeared and needing to hit one more ball in the hope that therein may lie the secret.

What a game!

You Only Have to Miss Once

I was a teenager when I first saw a performance of Paul Hahn Sr., the great touring trick-shot artist. The show was in Omaha, Nebraska, out on West Dodge at Pounders' Driving Range (what a great name for a driving range) owned by PGA pro Leon

Pounders. Hahn had not been in this kind of show business long, yet still arrived in his own private plane that he piloted. There have been more impressive ball strikers in the trick-shot field, but no one could touch Hahn's showmanship, timing of jokes, and handling of the audience. He was truly a master.

One of the closing highlights of the show was to have a local volunteer, who had already agreed to appear, be a part of a specialty shot. Paul would drive a golf ball from a tee held between the teeth of the subject while the volunteer was lying on the ground. In this case, the subject was Miss Nebraska, a very attractive young woman. To heighten the crowd's concern Paul would have an assistant put a black blindfold around his eyes while he was addressing the ball. It was tense, even intense, theater. He finally made the swing, hit a lovely shot, then tore off the blindfold and helped the young lady to her feet. He acknowledged the contribution of the volunteer to the audience as they applauded loudly, and as she exited he held up the blindfold, which revealed an eye hole for his left eye that supposedly had been covered. With the audience to his right they were unable to detect this ploy. It was still a risky shot. Soon after the Omaha engagement, his manager told Paul to drop that shot from his act. The most convincing argument was, *"You only have to miss once."*

WHAT'S THE VALUE IN WINNING AND IN LOSING?

When coaching a golf team or teaching individual golfers who are engaged in competition, I try to have them understand the real meaning of the terms "winner" and "loser." A winner is someone who gives it their best possible effort despite the odds or circumstances. A loser is someone who dogs it, quits, or gives less than their best. In a golf event there may be 124 players and only one is going to have the lowest score to earn a win. That doesn't make the rest of the field "losers." Many of them may have played their hearts out and scored well, maybe as well as they could, but someone else simply did better. To illustrate that point I have used this story.

In the days when UCLA seemed unbeatable in basketball and John Wooden was the magical mentor, the team made its annual Pac 10 visit to Eugene, Oregon, at McArthur Court. The Oregon Duck team was small and slow. I guess you could say kind of like ducks. Compared to UCLA's talent it was a classic mismatch: Pee Wee Herman vs. Andre the Giant. But sporting events occasionally have a strange way of defying the prognosticators and the odds-makers, especially when the underdog is the home team.

It was an epic battle that actually looked like it would end favoring the Ducks. With a few seconds to go, Oregon had a chance to ice the game with two shots from the foul line, but missed. UCLA scored in the last second to win by one point. As the Oregon Athletic Department's sports events manager I had spent the evening traversing the arena. But for the end of the game I found myself standing in the third balcony looking almost straight down on the floor when the final shot by UCLA went in. Fans left their seats, and coming up the aisle toward me I heard one man say, "Losers again!" I stood there stunned. Did he see the game I saw? Was he totally blind to the amazing gritty performance by a team that almost pulled off the upset of the decade? "Losers?" No way! The scoreboard or scorecard shows only the numbers. What it doesn't show is what was in your heart.

So what is the value in winning in sports and winning at golf? Or for that matter, what's the value in shooting a low score or having a low handicap? Does that impact the world in some positive way? Does it impact you in some positive way? In and of itself, NO. But winning can be a personal plus, if one or more of the following things happen to you:

1. Gain a healthy self-concept that assists you in accomplishing other things in your life.

2. Develop a greater respect for the value of effort and reward.

3. Learn to appreciate the contribution of a good mentor or coach in helping you to achieve a goal.

4. Use the recognition of your accomplishments as the chance to be a role model.

5. Add enjoyment to your life.

These apply to basketball, to golf, and to life in general.

You Just Can't See It All

I always cringe when I hear someone proclaim they have "the only way to do something," when in fact a casual investigation would prove them to be overstating their case. That is why in writing the *PGA Teaching Manual* one of the early quotes I used was from the great philosopher Nietzsche: "This is my way. What is your way? *The Way* doesn't exist." That is why golf gurus who come along claiming to have the only teaching method that is effective in learning how to play the game get the cold shoulder from me.

An example I use comes from a Buddhist meditation garden that contains 15 rocks of different sizes placed among white sand that has been raked in a wave pattern. What the garden represents is the mystery of life, for no matter where you stand in the garden you cannot see all of the stones. There are vantage points that allow you to see nine, or 11, or 12, and then when switching your position you can see rocks you couldn't see before, but now others are no longer in view. In the garden, just as in life, *no one can see it all*. Golf is the same in that respect.

The path leadng to the 15 rocks.

WELL MEANING DOES HAVE VALUE

I found myself in Sioux Falls, South Dakota, entered in an event at the Westward Ho Country Club, a stop on the Dakota Mini Tour. The 18-hole layout on the river flats offered a good challenge when the wind blew, which happened regularly.

For my playing exemption I was asked to give a clinic on Thursday evening and also play in the men's pro-am on Wednesday, which I was happy to do. On Tuesday morning came another request: could I also play in the women's pro-am that day? Although it was not part of my preparation plan, I agreed to the request and teed off with four high handicap women at 1:40 p.m. on a hot windy afternoon. It was a slow round. My team wasn't a threat to be competitive. While we carried on some conversation, they played their game and I played mine. There wasn't a lot I could do to help.

We came to the most difficult hole on the course, a 424-yard dogleg right around a pond. The wind would be blowing against us on our second shot, so I tried to hit my tee shot as close to the water on the right as I could…and I did. It rolled off the fairway, across the rough and into the hazard, but not into the water. The ball was resting on a dirt patch just out of the water. I could play it. The problem was that the ball was below my feet, the wind was blowing some 20 mph into me, the green was 188 yards away, plus a small tree about 50 yards ahead blocked my direct line. I chose to try to hit a cut 1-iron around the tree to get the ball going somewhere toward the green. It was risky, but I had little to lose. The shot ended up 10 feet from the hole, one of the best I have ever hit in my life. However, from my group I heard…*not a word*. They had just witnessed an amazing shot and they didn't even know it! Two putts later, after making a great par, it was on to the next hole, a short downwind 365-yarder.

I bombed the drive in the fairway, leaving me a 60-yard sand wedge to the flagstick. As I was about to play, the ladies' carts pulled up to watch. I forced my right hand into the shot rather than staying connected, pulled it 20 feet left of the flag and 30 feet past the cup. In unison they said, "Nice shot," and meant it! IT WASN'T A NICE SHOT! IT WAS A TERRIBLE SHOT! DON'T YOU UNDERSTAND ANYTHING ABOUT GOLF? Those thoughts raced through my mind as I suffered a slow burn. I wanted to get out of there and go practice, or just leave this group of stupid people. But you know what? They weren't stupid people; they were very nice people, a lot nicer than I was at that moment…and their comment on my previous shot was well-meaning. Why did I think because I could hit a golf ball better than they that I was something special? There must be dozens, maybe hundreds of tasks in which they could outdo me. Did that make me stupid? It was time to wake up to the fact that if you are a talented player of the game, any game, any activity, don't ever disparage those who can't match your particular skill. We all have some things we don't do as well as other people. So remember, when in the company of others less skilled than we are, and when demonstrating our specialty, it's always important to maintain a sense of humility.

Not Ahead of Its Time

Owning a company, Golf Around the World, which sells over 150 learning and training aids, I have seen many people's ideas of what they think is the perfect device to teach the swing. At our office in Lake Park, Florida, we are sent several of these products every month. After having been in business for quite a while, you start to think you've just about seen it all. But here was one that amazed me.

I received a call from a gentleman in California who said he had been working on a teaching aid that was going to revolutionize instruction. It would be used by every high school and college for their golf teams and golf instruction classes. He asked if I were coming to California soon so that I could see it. I wasn't. He said he was still working on improving it and would stay in touch. More than a year later the follow-up call came. I told him I still wasn't headed for California soon. As it turns out, he then wanted to come to Florida to demonstrate his invention to me. I tried to discourage this because of the expense, suggesting rather that he send some pictures and a description. We could start at that point to see if we had any interest. He was determined to travel, so we set aside a date. He also asked if there was a place at my home that had an electrical outlet and room enough to make a full swing so he could set up his equipment. There was, out on the back patio.

Our inventor pulled up in front of my house on the prescribed day accompanied by his wife, possibly for moral support. I could see the cost of this trip adding up with airfare, motel, car, and an extra person. The trunk of the Chevy was open because it contained a large, flat, wooden object, held in place by a rope. As I went out to greet him I couldn't help but think that the object strongly resembled half a ping-pong table. It was dark green with a white line running down the middle. The man was pleasant but businesslike. He wore glasses that gave him the look of a scientist.

We got right down to the task of preparing his demonstration out on the patio. The "half ping-pong-like table," which turned out to be only slightly smaller, was placed vertically on the brick floor like a backstop. A light green felt runner, some 12 to 15 feet long and about three feet wide, was placed at the base of the board. It ran back to an artificial grass mat that was obviously going to be a tee location. This was looking interesting, but not as interesting as it was about to be. I showed him the electrical outlet into which he attached a plug from a small hot pot. In the hot pot there were putty-like objects about the size and shape of golf balls that were wrapped in netting, similar to the kind you get around lemons at the grocery store. Completing the hot pot's contents was a liberal dose of talcum powder that was to attach itself to the ball-like objects once they were warmed.

When the warming process was complete, my visitor opened the pot, took out a couple of the net-covered "balls," placed one on the mat, and hit it with an iron so it struck the vertical green backstop in front of him. He then repeated the process with the second ball. In each case the "ball" would leave a powder spot where it struck the dark green surface, before it fell to the light green runner. Then came the shot's evaluation. The powder mark for the first ball made it evident it had struck on the left side of the white vertical line running down the middle of the green board. The initial shot direction was a pull. Where it landed on the mat indicated by the rebound direction, the ball's spin and whether it was a hook or slice. Now came the finale. Our inventor pulled out a rectangular piece of heavy poster board, 10"x4", into which were cut various-sized holes. He then held the board against the powder marks to assess their size in order to estimate the speed of the projectile hitting the board; the wider the mark, the faster the speed. It was an ingenious concept. But it was certainly not the final answer to the best practice device available to learn the golf swing. Keep in mind that we were already seeing in the marketplace reasonably-priced electronic equipment that was simple to operate and would give the user speed, path, timing, and face position when hitting shots.

When the demonstration was over, it was time for the obvious question: What did I think? We went into the house for a private conversation in the library. After asking him several questions about how much time he had spent on the project, the amount of money invested, his concept of marketing costs, and other things, I gave my honest answer: He should cut his losses and stop any further attempts at development because the product would never sell. His reaction was a mix of disappointment and anger. This was a proud man. He had previously successfully invented a product used worldwide with which you would be familiar if I were to share it with you. I could understand his response. We packed up and offered each other some perfunctory goodbyes. I never heard from him again. I felt badly, but the life lesson here is that *sometimes you have to be totally honest with people and not always try to placate them.* While it may be uncomfortable at the moment, for the long run it is in their best interest. It certainly was here.

On the Passing of Two Greats

Harry Vardon, six-time Open Champion and one of the immortals of the game, died in 1937. One of his contemporaries, J. H. Taylor, a member of the famous Great Triumvirate—Vardon, Braid and Taylor—gave these remarks concerning his great friend and competitor:

> I am often asked whom I consider to be the best golfer ever I saw, and, with a life experience behind me and having seen all the great players in the last 50 years, I give as my mature and considered judgment that Vardon was the greatest of them all.

> In addition to his wonderful skill, Harry Vardon will be remembered as long as the game lasts as one of the most courteous and delightful opponents that could ever be. I have good reason to appreciate this because

> Vardon and I, in the pursuit of our calling, met some hundreds of times; and although I was generally unsuccessful, I give it to him that when I was fortunate enough to win, he gave me the fullest possible credit.

Vardon negotiates a stymie.

Another tribute I should like to pay to my old friend —throughout the years I knew him, I never heard him utter one disparaging remark about any player. He was at all times most anxious with his help and advice. Allied to his magnificent skill, Harry Vardon will be always remembered as one of the most kindly souls that ever existed; and to know him was to love him.

J. H. Taylor, five-time British Open Champion, contemplating an unusual lie.

Note: J. H. Taylor, who wrote this tribute, was equally the match of Vardon not only as a player but also as a human being. I corresponded with his daughter, Phyllis, for several years, and received this note from her telling of what Lord Brabizon of Tara said at her father's funeral in 1963:

As long as the game of golf is played in every country in the world, the name of the great Englishman, John Henry Taylor, will be remembered. He set a standard of uprightness and honesty that raised the status of the professional golfer in society. He founded the PGA [The British PGA in 1901, 15 years before the U.S.] and was the first chairman. Mr. Taylor will be remembered not only as a golfer, but also as a man of strong and resolute character, unspoilt by success, whose manners were impeccable and who, although humble, would fight hard for a principle, or help less fortunate friends in the profession. His gentle courtliness never varied toward royalty or the most humble of his friends, and now we are gathered to say farewell to one of the very few people we meet in this world who could be called a real great man.

We should all aspire to eulogies equal to those of these two grand golfers.

A NUMBER TO REMEMBER

Jack Burke Jr. and I were team teaching a Resident School for the members of Omaha Country Club in Nebraska. Having spent a lifetime of being around the game's greats, Jackie was fascinating to listen to. He is a bit of philosopher as well as a great golf teacher and player. This is a story he shared with our class. "I went to a Catholic boys' high school with a lot of kids whose families weren't in the upper income brackets. On the first day of Sociology class, the priest came in, wrote his name on the corner of the blackboard, then drew a large circle in the middle of the board and wrote the number **59** inside the circle. He said, 'Boys, I want you to look very carefully at that number, study it, memorize it, and know it by heart, as it may be the most important number you will ever learn.' Then he sat down for about 10 minutes and told us to keep studying the number before he started the class. The next day he repeated the circle, the number **59,** and the previous day's instructions. We started to wonder what was going on. That feeling became particularly true after two more days of the same beginning for class. On Friday, he went through the same ritual but now he gave an explanation. 'Many of you young men have no training or experience in handling money. But if you apply yourself at this school you have a good chance to go out and make some good money for the first time. This number **59** is your personal economics lesson. No matter how well you do financially, remember one important rule: *if you make 59 you can't spend 60!'"*

A Man of His Word

Jackie Burke came from good stock. His father, Jack Burke Sr., was a fine player, finishing second in the 1920 U.S. Open by a stroke. Later in his career he won the PGA Seniors title. But he was more noted for being an excellent club professional, with most of his career served at River Oaks in Houston.

Prior to that location Jack Sr. was at Town and Country in St. Paul, Minnesota. He arranged for an exhibition match to be held there featuring the great Harry Vardon and Tom Vardon, Harry's brother who was the professional at the White Bear Yacht Club, and an excellent player in his own right. They were to play with Burke and his assistant, Eddie McGilligot. Posters were up and a large crowd was expected. The president of the club had been away when all of this was arranged. When he returned he heard of the event, saw the advertising, and went to the shop for a word with Burke. He approved of the event but did not want to have McGilligot as a part of the exhibition. He claimed that Eddie was not of the stature nor had the game of the other three. He may have been right, but Burke said that it had already been advertised and he personally had asked Eddie to play. The president made his wishes even stronger. Burke held his ground, saying he had made a promise. The president then fired his final salvo, "If McGilligot plays you can start looking for another job!" Then he left.

It was just a few years ago that I visited Eddie McGilligot in the White Palms Nursing Home in North Palm Beach, Florida. He was 83 years old and had enjoyed a long career as a head professional. He told me the story I just related and how after the match at Town and Country he had helped Jack Burke Sr. clean out the pro shop. Burke had remained true to his promise and that is how the Burke family happened to end up in Houston, Texas.

Jackie Burke and his beautiful swing.

Never Too Late

I haven't had a lot of golfing idols, but one person who does fit that category was Paul Runyan, the diminutive wonder from Hot Springs, Arkansas. He was always one of the shortest hitters on the Tour, yet he won The PGA Championship twice, was the leading money winner in 1933 and 1934, played on two Ryder Cup teams, and won three Senior PGA titles. So much for having to be a long driver!

It was an honor to be on the *Golf Digest* Professional panel with Paul. At a panel meeting in North Carolina we had 18 holes of golf scheduled at the end of the two-day gathering. I was paired with Paul, two-time U.S. Open champion Dr. Cary Middlecoff, and one of the *Golf Digest* writing staff, Larry Dennis. Paul did not have a lot of fun on the course that day. He was hitting it very short and his normally superb short game wasn't even enough to rescue him. When he finished he said to me, "Gary, I am playing so badly that I'm either going to quit the game or go back to work." Well Paul was not a quitter.

So at age 65 he went back to work, physical work and practice. In the early part of his career he was never a believer in using weights for physical training but he started to swing weighted objects, mostly things from the garage like a rake or shovel. Two years later at age 67 he entered a PGA Tour event, The Bob Hope Desert Classic, and shot three opening rounds of 75, 75, 75, beating several youngsters. The message? *It's never too late*.

He Had It Right

The PGA National Academy of Golf for Juniors attracted a great young golf talent out of Wales by the name of Phillip Parkin. Coming from a small town with a nine-hole course, he rose to the level of representing Wales in the World Cup. He also had a short stint on the PGA Tour before returning to Great Britain where he served as a golf television announcer for SKY TV.

Certainly a highlight for Phil, who became almost a part of our family, was playing in the Masters after winning the British Amateur. The season following his last year at the Academy brought him to Augusta and his opening day pairing was... Arnold Palmer. Phil was wearing his PGA Jr. Academy visor when he teed off on number one. Arnold had already hit his opening drive when Phil stepped to the tee. Phil's ball carried over the top of the hill on number one on the fly, some 50 yards past Palmer's. Arnold turned to the gallery and said, "Where do they get these kids?"

The most impressive part about Phillip was not his amazing golf; it was his freshness, honesty, and character. Spanking new to the United States, he was genuinely surprised and amazed at things he had never seen before—like any kind of drive-in, bank, cleaners, or drugstore. Phil was honest to a fault, believing totally what anyone said because telling the truth was how one was supposed to live. As for Phillip's character, let me share this story.

We were in an evening program at the golf camp. Phil was sitting in the back row of the tiered classroom. As a part of our values orientation at the camp I read the following story as a case study on honesty:

> It is the High School State Championship Golf Tournament. The team from Springfield High is one of the best in years. The timing for a possible championship

run is perfect, as their coach is retiring after this season, having lead the 'Cougars' in golf for 23 years. He had a lot of good teams and several All-State individual players, but never had won the state team title.

After the first day of the 36-hole event the Cougars were one shot off the lead and they hadn't yet played up to their potential. But on the final day they started to click and by the time their first three players were in they showed a two shot lead. All that was left was for their number one player, Scott, to continue the good golf he had shown in the first nine holes. But on the 16th, a dogleg left around some woods and out-of-bounds, he pulled his tee shot into the trees. It could possibly be 'out' if it took a bad kick. After the other two players in his group pushed their tee shots to the right rough, he played a provisional ball. But this one was worse, a diving hook that was definitely beyond the O.B. stakes. His next provisional was pushed well to the right near his playing partner's drives.

They went to locate their shots while Scott began a worried search for his original ball, a Titleist #4. Racing through his mind were the thoughts of letting his team down. If both balls were gone he would be lying five and facing a quadruple bogey. There would go the championship and with it the possibility of a personal scholarship, since the individual title, which seemed so attainable only a few minutes before, would be gone as well. Then he spotted it, a Titleist #4, it was playable, and in bounds. He selected his club and visualized a possible recovery shot that would put him near the green. But as he prepared to hit his shot, he looked more closely at the ball and realized that while it was nearly the same as his, it wasn't his. It was a slightly different model. What should he do?

That was the question that was posed to the 66 teenage boys and girls who were sitting in front of me. I now asked for their response as to what Scott should do. The answers began to come:

"Play it! Nobody's going to find out."

"Well, I wouldn't cheat for myself, but I would so the coach could get the title."

"Heck, nobody would know about it but you, and your team really deserved to win."

And then from other students: "But how would you feel if you accepted the trophy and knew that you cheated?"

"What if you were the second-place team and found out that the winner had cheated to win?"

Then Phillip raised his hand and when I recognized him he said, "I don't understand the question." In that statement was revealed the highest degree of our camp's value of honesty. In Phillip's mind there was absolutely no question, you simply play by the rules.

You never know when a kid in the audience will turn out to be a star.

"You May Not Remember Me..."

My family and I once lived two blocks from the University of Oregon in a nice home surrounded mostly by various types of student housing including apartments. Next door on one side was a house that had seen much better days before it started being rented to groups of students who came and went with little concern for their habitat.

It rained a great deal during the winter months in the Willamette Valley. But when spring rolled around and the windows were opened to the kinder weather, that's when the distinct fragrance of marijuana would waft over across my driveway from our neighbors. It was Vietnam War time, and long hair, tattoos, beads and tie-dye were in style, particularly next door.

A lovely golf day was in store for me. I was dressed in my plus fours, standing on the front lawn of my house, waiting with my clubs for my ride to pick me up. I decided to make some practice swings to refresh what I had been thinking about as a playing thought for the day. While I was swinging, one of the hippies from next door wandered over. It was around noon but he was just getting up and looked it. Bare feet, jeans with the stylish holes in the knees and a wrinkled T-shirt left little doubt that he had probably slept in his clothes. He asked me, "Are you going out to play?" I told him I was. We then got into a discussion about the game. He indicated he had played a bit when he was younger (that couldn't have been too long ago) and that he enjoyed it at the time. That is about all I remember about the conversation except that he seemed more likeable after talking with him than I would have imagined from his looks.

Twenty-five years later I received a very nice letter that started, "You may not remember me but…" it was the young man from next door who was writing. He related some of his personal story, referring to his life at the time we talked and since. Yes, he was into drugs then and not doing well in school. But there was something in our conversation that got him to make an attempt to turn things around. He was now enjoying a successful life, marriage, and family. Seeing my picture in a golf magazine gave him a means to get in touch, and he just wanted to let me know how helpful our conversation was that day on my front lawn. I have absolutely no recollection of attempting to lift his spirits, or preach any message to that young man. But something was said that did. It is a grand example of how small human kindnesses, even just words, can make a difference.

Living Up to Commitments

It was always a joy to contact a famous golfer from The Tour and get a "yes" response when asking them to do a one-day presentation for our PGA National Academy of Golf for Juniors in Boca Raton, Florida. This was especially true when there were so many outstanding people who agreed to help us: Dr. Gil Morgan, Julius Boros, Calvin Peete, Craig Stadler, Barbara Romack, Ben Crenshaw, Tom Kite, Larry Nelson, "Chick" Harbert, Dow Finsterwald, Hubert Green, Peter Jacobson, Dennis Walters, Jay Hebert, and Lon Hinkle. However there was one player I would have to say went "the second mile," and that was Andy North. All of the players came for no fee, giving of their services freely. But Andy's was a special case. He had been scheduled to appear in June, on a Tuesday, the week after the U.S. Open and the week of the Canadian Open. Andy's career had yet to list any PGA Tour victories, although he was a respected player. More importantly to us, he was a good role model for young people.

The U.S. Open was being contested at Cherry Hills in Denver, a two-hour time zone difference for us in Florida. To the golfing world's surprise and our campers' as well, North was leading the tournament on Sunday. The kids in the camp were going crazy, knowing that he would be arriving in two days. Then, coming into the final holes, Andy's swing started to leak oil. He hit a combination of marginal and poor shots that cut his lead to one stroke coming to the last hole. The whole camp was around the TV set after our dinner and before evening activities that started at 7 p.m.

The 18th hole at Cherry Hills is a long dogleg left par-4, and there was a gusty wind blowing. Andy needed to par it for victory. His drive was not good. He tried to recover with a strong 2-iron but pulled it into the left greenside bunker. He now faced a tough bunker shot that he needed to get up and down to win. After some deliberation he blasted out to around five feet. You can imagine the level of tension in the TV room at the camp among the students and staff watching North line up his putt. He got set…then backed off. Everybody groaned. "Now he'll never make it," I could hear one of the campers say. Andy got set a second time…and backed off again! More groans, hand-wringing, visor-pulling, and head-shaking. Then he stepped up and rolled it into the cup. There followed an eruption of emotion not only in Denver at 5 p.m. mountain time, but also in Boca Raton at 7 p.m. as the students ran out to their evening intramural activity program.

There was extra excitement that night during intramurals with the thought of an Open Champion coming soon. But as the activity ended and the campers were heading toward the evening lecture there arose some uncertainty. Comments such as, "He's just won the U.S. Open. He's not coming to a junior golf camp" floated around. While it was campers who made the comments, it certainly started to enter my mind as well. But here is what happened.

Andy North had just won his first tournament as a PGA Tour player, a Major, the big one, the U.S. Open. Obviously he spent that evening and way into the night on phone calls and celebration. He was committed to an event the next day, Monday, in the Detroit area for a luncheon to be followed by an afternoon golf outing. When Andy arrived in Detroit he talked, played, and of course was inundated with people wanting to hear more about his experience. It was a long day. Now it was decision time. He was scheduled to fly that night to West Palm Beach. I was to pick him up and drive him to camp in Boca Raton for his full day plus an evening on Tuesday, where he was to give a clinic and talk to a group of junior golfers. His next playing event was starting Thursday, the Canadian Open, in Toronto, almost within spitting distance of Detroit by air, but not from Florida. He'd get

Andy North, a man of his word.

neither rest nor a practice round of any consequence for the Canadian Open if he went to Florida…but he came. Yes, he was tired. Yes, I'm sure he would rather have been somewhere else, but he made a commitment and he lived up to it. As I think back on it I still marvel at his loyalty and his class. Would it happen today? I leave that up to you to decide.

Let me close with a footnote. At the afternoon clinic, when North had finished giving a demonstration and was now sitting in a director's chair under a tent surrounded by 66 campers plus staff, he was asked, "Why did you back away twice on that putt?"

Andy responded that the wind was blowing and his being tall was causing him to lose balance over the putt and so he backed off until he could feel steady. "After all," he said, "You don't have many opportunities to win the U.S. Open with a five-foot putt and I wanted to give it my best."

Then came the final comment from a then 13-year-old, and now current LPGA touring pro, Kris Tschetter. Kris said, "Mr. North, I don't have a question. I just wanted to say that if you had backed away from that putt once more we would have been late for intramurals." It was a great comment that Andy never forgot, and it sealed a casual friendship between the two that has lasted years later…Andy North, you are a class act.

So What's *Your* Handicap?

Golfers seem to worry a lot about their handicaps. While we all want to live up to our potential, we must admit that it is pretty much an ego thing. When I ask a student who is a 15 handicap what he/she would like to achieve, I very often get the reply, "A single digit handicap." But we all should be grateful for what we do have, and that is the capacity to play without the kind of challenge that faced Tommy McAuliffe, the armless golfer pic-

tured here. I have included these photos to serve as a reminder
that we have quite a bit less of a handicap to overcome than
others. As it says in the picture, *"An Inspiration to Mankind."*

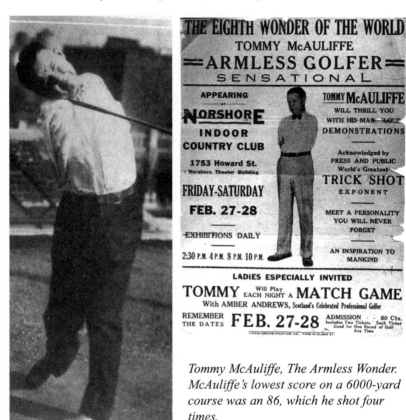

Tommy McAuliffe, The Armless Wonder.
McAuliffe's lowest score on a 6000-yard
course was an 86, which he shot four
times.

WHAT A PUTT!

I have always wanted to know how much money golf raises for
charity nationwide in an entire year. It must be enormous when
you think of all the events, large and small. One such event on
the smaller side that I have been instrumental in creating is the
Martha Lloyd School Charity Classic. Troy, Pennsylvania, home
of the school, is a one-stoplight town 27 miles south of Elmira,
New York. The single stoplight may suggest to you the size of its
population but not the size of its heart, for the town contains a

host of loving people who take care of the physically- and mentally-challenged residents of the school. A local woman, Martha Lloyd, established the school in 1928, after having searched for help with her mentally-handicapped daughter and finding none.

The charity golf event is held at Corey Creek G. C. just outside of Mansfield, Pennsylvania, about 20 miles west of Troy. Art Connelly has been the pro in perpetuity, or so it seems, and makes things work at the event along with PGA member Jim Edmister from Elmira and Martha Lloyd president, Dick MacIntire. My job has been to entertain the major donors at a cocktail party the night before the tournament, give a clinic the next day prior to people teeing off, then play and hand out prizes.

The second year of the event was a beautiful day at Corey Creek, and the participants were in a good mood. We were having a participatory clinic with the entrants featuring the short pitch shot around the practice green. After they all had taken several attempts aided by verbal coaching, I brought them up on the green for a short putting demonstration. This is what I said:

"I want to thank you for supporting this event; it is a great cause. We can come out and enjoy the wonderful game of golf, but the residents of Martha Lloyd, due to their limitations, are unable to do that. Your participation here is helping these ladies have a better life. One of the residents is here today representing the school. Her name is Bryn, and she has been practicing her putting in her residence at the school just getting ready for today. She is with her mother over there. C'mon down, Bryn, and bring your putter." Bryn was 35 years old but is small and looks to be more like 12. She has a bright smile and sparkling personality but has limited motor skills, neurological damage from surgery at birth, and her sight is limited. I introduced her to the crowd and told them, "She has two older sisters who are good golfers, one an all-conference player when in high school. She also has a brother who is accomplished in the sport. However,

Bryn most likely will never be able to play the game, but she is here today to see how well she can do after her practice."

I then helped Bryn take her putting grip. We made a practice putt together with my arms reaching around her from the back. On the warm-up stroke we were going to no target, just getting the feel of the swing. Then we moved over to try a 10-foot, up-hill, right-to-left putt. The crowd got very quiet. I helped her with the aim, we stroked it together, and the ball rolled right into the cup. The audience broke into animated cheering and applause. Bryn beamed! Then I turned to the group as I placed my arm around her shoulder. When they had quieted, I said, "Ladies and gentlemen, I would like to introduce you to my daughter, Bryn Wiren."

Just a Spoonful of Sugar

It has always been important to me in my teaching to try and emphasize the fun element in golf. Having fun is a must when working with juniors. Playing games, having contests, challenges, even doing things like picking up the range balls should be made enjoyable. In the accompanying photo you will see a junior class sprinting out on my whistle to see how many balls they can gather in their buckets before the signal to stop. It was an activity that was part of the values training at Oakway. But it was conducted in a way that was enjoyable. When you look at the picture you can see they are having a good time. While doing it they learned about rules.

Rule #1: You must have your foot touching the range wall until the start signal is given.

Rule #2: If a single whistle is heard while picking up, you had to freeze the position of your body until another whistle sounded.

Rule #3: When the final double whistle blew you could not pick up any more balls, even if your hand was almost upon one.

Rule #4: You were to count the results of your effort and stand at attention, step forward and announce your total. Report no more, no fewer, just as you would your golf score...it is a game of honesty.

Winners got rewards in the pro shop and non-winners played a finger counting game for a wildcard win. The lesson is simple. Make it fun and they will come.

Even picking up balls can be made fun.

PUTTING IT IN PERSPECTIVE

Golfers with a high degree of skill and success can develop an overblown sense of their own importance. Helping put a golfer's achievements in perspective is this essay written in 1978 by Patrick Caton, 10 years of age, in Bermuda.

"Dimples..."

I was feeling rather embarrassed. Here I was, an adventurous golf ball sitting in a shop window with everyone staring at me. I would rather be knocked about a golf course than sitting here doing nothing.

It was nearing my third day in the shop window when I was bought. I thought I would finally see a golf course. The buyer took me to his house and put me in a golf bag. I found another golf ball who told me that there was a golf tournament the next day. I then fell into contented sleep, thinking that at last I would see a golf course.

At the tournament I was taken out of the bag and teed off with a mighty "Whack." I sailed down the fairway and landed with a thump on the grass. My owner came up and sailed me away again and again.

After the first few holes I was feeling sore. I was dirty and exhausted from those mighty "Whacks and Thumps." I wanted to rest but my owner wouldn't allow me. I just had to score hole after hole. As I neared the 18th hole, I felt that I was going to fall apart. I was not used to the rough treatment. With a last "Whack"—I landed within two inches from a 10-foot putt. My owner putted me into the hole and took me out again. The spectators cheered wildly, whistled, and stomped their feet. When I looked around and saw this, I muttered slowly to myself, "I do all the work and he gets all the credit."

Author's Note: So, if any of us happen to temporarily master the game, remember—nothing is ever accomplished alone!

GOLF ENJOYMENT SCORECARD

The opening line of the first book I wrote (**Golf: Building a Solid Game**, 1970) was, *"Golf is a game and as such is meant to be enjoyed."* For many golfers the game is filled with too much pain and frustration and too little joy. The primary reason for this is that they have limited their concept of enjoyment to one criterion: the score. Ask them if they had a good time and the answer comes only after they add up the numbers on the card. Putting all our eggs into the basket of scoring reduces the chance of enjoyment considerably because we only play as well as we think we should about 10-20% of the time. That return is too low when considering the amount of time, effort, and money that is being invested in what is supposed to be a pleasurable experience.

In considering this problem I asked myself, how do we know when we have had a good time at golf or anything for that matter? Let's use the example of coming home from a party with your spouse and turning to him/her with the following comment. "Wasn't that a good time tonight?" What made it that way? Was it the food, the location, the facility, the entertainment, the program, the people you met, the conversations you had? More than likely it was a combination of several things. That should be the way it is in golf, as there are a variety of elements that could influence one's opinion about the experience. So what I have done is to create a **Golf Enjoyment Scorecard** to help a person identify those possibilities for pleasure in the game beyond the score.

To find out what combination of elements in the game give you the most satisfaction, look at the list of 10 that have been compiled. Rate each one with a percentage of importance to you. The total of the 10 must be equal to and not exceed 100%. For example, Course Design may be something that you really pay little attention to when playing the game and therefore may rate it low at 5%. On the other hand, if you are an aficionado of that subject you might give it 20%. So rate the factors as to how important they are to you in having an enjoyable time. Keep in mind, however, you only have a total of 100% with which to work.

Golf Enjoyment Scorecard

ELEMENTS	PERCENTAGE
1. Design of the Course: Variety of holes, the challenge, memorability, fairness	_____%
2. Course Conditioning: Greens, fairways, roughs, bunkers, tees	_____%
3. Aesthetics of the Course: Terrain, trees, views, setting, flowers, water	_____%
4. Amenities: Staff, clubhouse, lockers, food and beverage, carts, range, caddies	_____%
5. The People with Whom You Play: Friends, customers, family, competitors, people with whom you have been paired	_____%
6. Weather: Perfect, cold, hot, windy, rainy	_____%
7. Your General Overall Performance: How well you managed the course and yourself, hit some good shots, stayed focused, appreciated your own efforts	_____%
8. Competition: Won or lost your match, a tournament, bets	_____%
9. Exercise: Walked nine or 18 holes, pulled a cart, carried your bag	_____%
10. Score: What you shot, the final number on the card	_____%
Total:	**100%**

As you review the 10 elements you will find there is something deeper here than "Grip It and Rip It," than "Never Up Never In," or "Whadya shoot?" something of the spirit...but only if you look for it. Otherwise golf can be a lifetime exercise of semi-frustration over not quite being what we think we could be, caught up in the siren song of the temptress of scoring. That's when we have forgotten that golf is really in the Toy Department of life, the department that can bring joy to the soul and refreshment to the spirit.

IT IS MY SINCERE HOPE IN CREATING THIS ENJOYMENT SCORECARD THAT PLAYERS WILL RECOGNIZE THAT THERE ARE IMPORTANT ELEMENTS OF THE GAME BEYOND SCORE THAT ARE WORTHY OF APPRECIATION AND CAN CONTRIBUTE SUBSTANTIALLY TO ENJOYMENT OF THE GAME.

#9. Exercise...You don't have to ride in the golf cart, only rent it.

The beauty of golf is something to celebrate.

RAKs

Before this chapter on "Golf Brings a Special Message" reaches its final example, I would like to mention a subject that comes up in many talks that I give to golfing groups. That subject is RAKs, or Random Acts of Kindness. I see golf as a game of civility, a quality that is being gradually lost in our society, a society that encourages a "trash-talking," "in your face," "win at all costs" sports environment. In golf we honor our opponent and appreciate him/her as a cooperating competitor, there to help us test and demonstrate our skills. In that kind of environment RAKs naturally happen, but what about beyond golf?

A Random Act of Kindness is one in which someone does something for another human being with no thought of reward or recognition. This title was created when a person driving on the freeway during rush hour in San Francisco stopped to pay the toll and gave the attendant enough to pay for the next six cars following. When those six people pulled up to pay and were told, "Your toll has been paid by a car ahead of you," think of the reaction. A ray of sunshine just appeared in what may have been a tough day for the RAK recipient. It may have given hope. It may have changed an attitude. It may have made a difference. You never know for sure about RAKs, except that they are not unimportant.

After giving this talk on RAKs to the Tommy Armour Golf Company at their annual sales meeting, encouraging those in attendance to add this element to their lives, I received this anecdote. Jeff Matheson, a salesperson and later executive with the company, told of stopping in a sports memorabilia card shop to get a baseball card for his son. While he was there, a mother pushing a boy of about 12 in a wheelchair entered the store. The young man made a request for a card to which the mother had to say no as that card was apparently beyond their budget. Ready to leave the store after his purchase, Jeff thought of the RAK talk. He quietly asked the clerk about the card, paid for it, telling him to give it to the boy, and left the store. Jeff went next door to another store. As he was leaving that store, the woman and her son were coming out of the memorabilia store, the boy smiling and holding the card in his hand. Jeff said, "It made my day even more than I think it made his."

Here is an RAK in the form of a kind word and pat on the back from PGA Pro Derek Hardy.

There are many chances for those of us who play golf to extend our civility and compassion beyond the golf course into the rest of our lives. *Look for opportunities to provide Random Acts of Kindness, and you will experience a joy far greater than the satisfaction that comes from a well-played round.*

OBSERVATIONS AND QUIPS

You don't need 20 million dollar clubhouses, or a 30 million dollar golf course to enjoy the game. These are merely trappings. I can't remember having any more fun than when I was a kid, playing a 1,976 yard par-33, dirt tee, nine-hole muny course with my friends for 10 cents a hole. The greens fees were $1.75 for adults and 35 cents for kids. It had no practice range, not even a practice putting green. God alone watered the course except for some help by me, the night waterboy, who assisted Him on the greens. Spring Lake was the farthest thing from fancy, but it was golf. You played from point A to point B, ending at a 4¼-inch target, while trying like heck to see if you could do better than the next guy, or to improve on your score from last time. It was in its simplest form, the game. It's the essence of simplicity that captivates anyone called "a golfer."

It's the game, not the trappings, that hooks the kids.

Although princes, kings, prime ministers, millionaires, military leaders, the rich and the famous have all been members of the Royal and Ancient Golf Club, there is only one plaque of recognition that is attached to the building. It is to a golf professional, "Old Tom" Morris, 1821-1908. It was said of Tom in his eulogy, "That he never had an enemy."

Speaking of old men, an old golf professional was approached by a young man who told his elder that he would like to be a golf pro.

"Is that so?" said the veteran pro. "Let me ask you a question, son."

"Yes, sir," said the young man.

"Do you know why the word *business* is longer than the word *golf*?"

"No sir, I don't."

"Well it's because if you don't pay attention to the big word, you won't be in the small one."

Gary Player has made it a lifelong habit to excuse himself from conversations turning negative.

The greatest teachers of golf are not only teachers of mechanics, but also teachers of life. Harvey Penick, the soft-spoken, humble-beyond-words, totally dedicated to helping others Texan, would epitomize that statement.

You can't always control the result of a golf shot. The perfectly-struck ball may hit the flagstick and carom into a bunker. But you can control your reaction to it.

Golf looks deceptively easy. You know what? It isn't. Golf is like a Charlie Chaplin movie, part comedy, part tragedy. It takes you from Mr. Everest to Death Valley all in the same day, or even the same hole.

QUOTES

"Golf is a bloodless sport…if you don't count the ulcers." **Dick Schaap**

"You don't have the game you played last year, or even last week. You have only today's game. It may be far from your best, but when that's all you've got, harden your heart and make the best of it." **Walter Hagen**

"There are no blind holes the second time you play them." **Tommy Armour**

"Pain and some suffering are inevitable in golf. But misery is a choice." **Chip Beck**

"Nothing goes down slower than a golf handicap." **Bobby Nichols**

"I didn't realize how much confidence meant in this game, until I didn't have any." **Bob Tway**

"Every man has his own inward dream about his own game, and about what he is really capable of—or would be, if only he had the time and opportunity to practice like a professional. The fact that he never lives up to it tarnishes the perfection of his private deal not one iota." **John Stobbs**

"Sometimes when a golfer with money meets a golfer with experience, the golfer with experience ends up with the money and the golfer with the money ends up with experience." **Anonymous**

*"The man who can putt is a match for anyone." Willie Park Jr. 1893
(He might have included women as well. It looks like this lady would putt
you for all that is in her purse).*

CHAPTER

6

There Are Many Bad Golf Jokes and Stories... But Here Are Some Good Ones

We have all sat through some "yawners" where the guy who can't tell a story begins one you have heard too many times and it wasn't any good when it was told well. I hope you will find the following stories new to your experience. Some are true and some are not. I leave you to decide which is which.

HE GOT HIS THREE CENTS WORTH

It was a "drech" day in 1898 at the Aberdeen Golf Club in Scotland. A Scottish "drech" day is when the temperature is hovering around 35 degrees Fahrenheit, the wind is coming in at 15 mph and there is a light rain falling. Nonetheless, being a hardy lot, the Scots don't ignore the links; in fact they find this kind of weather more of a challenge. Even so, on this day there were only a few groups so far who had come to play and one of the adult caddies had yet to get a bag. As the time was moving along toward noon, he took out his pocket watch, checked the time and thought he just might be slipping away to the pub for a "wee drinkie." But just then a member came over the hill and announced, "I'll be havin' a caddy." The only problem was that the man was the meanest, stingiest member of the whole damned club. But it could be the only chance for our caddy to go out, so he took the member's bag. Slinging the bag over his shoulder, he trudged off in his long Macintosh coat, flat woolen cap, and boots. He appeared ready for the weather.

But the weather turned worse. The temperature dropped a couple of degrees, the wind picked up 10 more mph, and the rain came down harder to make it a horrible day. All this added to the fact that the member shot 124 for 18 holes, having hit the ball repeatedly into the gorse, the heather, and the whins. When the round was completed, the caddy set the bag down and the member went into it to take out a long leather purse, the kind with two snaps at the top. The caddy, who was wet from his feet to his "arse," put out his hand for payment and got the flat bare minimum fee. Seeing the amount and considering the day, he looked at the member with a real glare in his eye, which caused the member to have a twinge in his Scottish heart. So he went back into the purse and came up with a three-penny tip, the large copper pennies of a day long ago.

When he placed them in the caddy's still outstretched hand, the caddy looked at those three pennies and then gazed intently at the member. He said, "Sir, I can be tellin' your fortune with these three pennies."

"And what that might be?" said the member.

With that the caddy began his fortune-telling. "Well, the first penny tells me that yer a Scot."

"Aye man, but ya know that already," said the member.

"But the second penny tells me that yer a bachelor," responded the caddy.

"Aye man, yer right, I am a bachelor," cried the surprised member.

The caddy increased his glaring look while making this final observation, "And the third penny tells me that yer father was also a bachelor!"

A Visit to the Islands

A rather unkempt scruffy looking post middle-aged man walked into the general manager's office of a large country club. After having been seated, he said that he was looking for a job.

"What kind of job?" asked the manager.

"Anything. Bag room, kitchen help, grounds, janitorial—just a job," he said.

"What's your name?" asked the G.M.

"Al," was his reply.

"What's the rest of your name?" was, of course, the next question.

"It's just plain Al," responded the applicant.

"You must have a last name," prodded the manager.

"Well I used to have one. I was Al Dingle Dangle. And I didn't have to come looking for menial jobs like this. You see, after finishing Columbia University, I went to Harvard Medical School and got a M.D. degree. So I was Al Dingle Dangle, M.D. I practiced successfully for several years around New York City but got bored with what I was doing so I decided to go to night school and took courses in history until I received a Ph.D. from NYU. That allowed me to do some occasional teaching in their history department. So then I was Al Dingle Dangle M.D., Ph.D. During a break in my schedule I took a trip to the Caribbean and met a sweet young girl with whom I spent a very enjoyable week. When I got back to New York I began having some physical problems, went to a fellow doctor, and found out I had V.D. When the AMA found out I had V.D., they took away my M.D., and when the AAUP found out I had V.D. they took away my Ph.D. and the V.D. took away my dingle dangle, so now I'm just plain Al." [This was one of the favorite stories of the great golf trick shot performer, Paul Hahn Sr.]

What a Way to Die

Former U.S. Open Champion Lou Graham is one heck of a nice guy. He tells of a moment when he wasn't so sure he'd be around anymore to demonstrate that Tennessee sweetness. Arriving a couple of days ahead of the Tour event in which he was about to compete, Lou was having a casual practice round. The usual pre-tournament activities were taking place: the last minute marking of the course, finishing up the corporate tents, roping off areas, and putting out the Port-a-Pottys. Some of those portable "johns" while waiting to be positioned had temporarily been placed on a bridge that traversed a large stream on the course. The side railings on the bridge were low, and the johns were standing vertically against them. Having to cross the bridge to the next tee, Lou, in need of a Potty's use, saw this as an opportunity to not have to hunt further for a relief station. He slipped inside to do his business while motioning his playing companions to go ahead to the tee. Maybe it was because he was going to be seated, or possibly his mother had told him to always lock the door when you go into the bathroom so no one is embarrassed. Whatever the thought process, Lou secured the door with some effort, using one of those old hook and eye fasteners. When he finished he tried to unfasten the latch. It wouldn't budge. Afraid of hurting his hand, he had a stroke of genius (he thought). Taking off one of his spiked shoes, he swung it upward to hit the hook and dislodge it from the eyehole. A couple of tries failed to move it, so he decided to put more effort behind the strike. That produced a mighty swing, but it was a whiff, an air shot. He missed his target entirely. The force of the swing hurled him backward against the john wall, which tipped it over the rail so that it was precariously balancing above the water. The thought flashed through Lou's mind

Former U.S. Open Champion Lou Graham

that in the next day's sports page the headline would be *"U.S. Open Champ drowns in Port-a-Potty."* Fortunately, before anything tragic occurred the structure was righted, he manipulated the hook to escape, and everyone was very relieved—especially Lou, in more ways than one. He later admitted that the final shoe effort was the worst swing he made that week.

A ROOKIE SPECTATOR

It has always been interesting to read about how many people watch golf on television who are fans but not golfers themselves. I suppose it is easier to do when you latch onto a superstar player like Tiger Woods or Anika Sorenstam and get emotionally involved with his or her performance. That certainly was the case for many fans of Arnold Palmer. He attracted a literal "Army" of people, both to their TV sets and to the course, to watch him hitch his pants after a good shot, or grimace in pain after a poor putt. One such non-playing fan lived near Arnie's hometown, Latrobe, Pennsylvania. The PGA Tour was playing an event in the Philadelphia area, so this fan decided he would drive down on the weekend and see his golf hero in person for the first time. He was not yet aware as to how personal it was going to be.

On noting in the paper that Arnold had made the cut and was in contention, our fan saw Arnold's starting time and picked Sunday for his first-ever experience of being on a golf course. He allotted adequate time to watch Arnold tee off…he thought…but missed it by 20 minutes, as his calculations did not include the traffic and remote parking that put him behind on his schedule. Once inside the gates, he stood there with a pairings sheet and course map in hand looking bewildered. Some kind soul judged from the look on our fan's face that there was a problem and went over to see if he could help. After hearing the man's plight and realizing it was his first time on a course, let alone at a tournament, he offered a suggestion. Palmer was probably about on the second green, which was pretty far away, but his group would be coming back this direction on the fourth hole. If our fan would walk down to where the Good Samaritan showed him, he could arrive early enough to get a spot along the fairway before the crowds got there and then be able to see his hero.

The Arnie fan took the advice and directions, locating the fourth fairway where there was still plenty of first-row room behind the ropes. After waiting for about 20 minutes he felt Mother Nature calling. It had been a long drive and not wanting to be late, he hadn't stopped along the way. Now, even though the other spectators were starting to fill up the viewing spaces, he needed to answer the call. There were some Port-a-Lets not far away in the rough and that was where he headed.

Arnold didn't make them all.

He was in there for a while. Just before opening the door to leave he heard some commotion outside. As he pushed the weathered door open there was a loud creaking sound like you hear from an old rusty hinge on a door that is opened in a mystery thriller. He was temporarily blinded by the sunlight that was directly in his eyes, but not so blinded that he didn't see the figure of his hero, Arnold Palmer, not more than 10 feet away, in his address position apparently ready to hit a recovery shot from the rough after a hooked drive. Palmer's head snapped up, staring irritably back at the location of the loud noise.

Quickly realizing the situation, our fan said, "Excuse me, Mr. Palmer," and pulled the door back shut. This wasn't exactly how he had planned to meet his idol.

The crowd quieted and then a murmur started up again, followed by a knock on the door. "This is Arnold Palmer," came the voice through the door. "Would you please come out? I can't concentrate on my shot while thinking of you standing in there."

Our fan pushed open the creaking door, apologized again, then slipped into the crowd; he could hardly go unnoticed as people were pointing him out and saying, *"There goes the guy in the Port-a-Let."*

THE MOST IMPORTANT PLACE

This is an approximate version of a story that Tommy Bolt related in his book *The Hole Truth* when he replied to the question: "What is the most important hole on a golf course?" Tommy answered that the "most important" is not a hole but a place. That place is the first tee, where you make the arrangements. You can be a Tiger Woods "play alike," but if you give too many stokes or don't take enough, you have already lost before you have begun. Bolt went on to give an example.

There was this industrialist in Southern California who had a successful business but a life without golf, until age 50. Once he started playing he didn't just "take up the game"—he inhaled it. Golf became a burning passion. After the first two years of "playing around" wherever he could get a game, he joined a club, or rather he joined THE club. No, not the most prestigious club in L.A., but the one where you could get the most action if you loved to gamble.

Our businessman would practice in the afternoons during

Tommy Bolt knew the most important place.

the week and play in the big games on the weekend. Because he had some athletic talent he became a respected player at the club. But at age 63, while on the course, he had a heart attack and could not be resuscitated in time. His family was in shock over his death, but even more so when they went to the attorney's office to hear the reading of the will. It said: "Dear Family and friends, It may surprise you to learn that I leave you no money. I had few vices in life, but one of them was gambling at golf. Though I leave you little, I die a happy man, having achieved a three handicap at my club. Nonetheless, I do have a last request. Please cut up my body into 18 pieces and bury one on each of the holes of the course I so dearly loved." End of will.

The attorney looked up to see the unbelieving faces of his gathering, when a slip of paper fell from the will onto the floor. He bent over, picked it up, and then read it to the audience. It said, "P.S. Bury my ass on the first tee 'cuz that's where I lost it."

MUIRFIELD'S PROTECTOR GENERAL

If someone ever suggested that the United Kingdom had a golf club/secretary who protected the sanctity of their course any more fervently than Capt. Paddy Hanmer at Muirfield, I would be hard-pressed to believe it. He was a legend in curmudgery.

Visitors who had made all the proper arrangements to play the course still would often stand trembling in his presence wondering if he would grant them the privilege to play.

So it is understandable why an American golfer, who was traveling to Scotland and wanted to play Muirfield, sought the backing of some USGA heavyweights to insure his acceptance. He was from a very well established club and had a respectable handicap but nonetheless solicited letters of introduction from a host of prominent people in golf, ranging from Joseph Dey Jr. (USGA Executive Director) in the East to Sandy Tatum (past USGA president) in the West.

The arrangements, including date and time, were made well in advance with all of the letters duly submitted. When our golfer arrived at the fabled links located just beyond the golf courses at Gullane, he presented himself to Hanmer. He gave his name and said that he was anticipating playing that day. Hanmer, in an annoyed manner, shuffled through papers as though he had just now, for the first time, heard of the request. Finally, he came upon the sheaf of letters and the American's golfing bio and after a grumble and an "hrumph" said, "Ah yes…most *'overcredentialed'* person I have ever seen!"

NEED TO LOOK IN THE RIGHT PLACE

It might sound silly to say, "Marion Heck is a heck of a golfer," but he is. Now a Floridian, he has had his moments playing with "the greats," on the PGA Tour and the Senior Tour before the name was changed to Champions Tour. But this story isn't about the Tours; it is about a casual round with some friends at the Old Marsh Golf Club in Palm Beach Gardens, Florida. Old Marsh is a fine course that also features a display in its clubhouse of an outstanding antique golf club collection purchased from Laurie Auchterlonie of St. Andrews.

A pleasant day, a good foursome, a wonderful course and amenities, what more could you want? Well one thing…a faster group playing in front of you. Since the fifth hole it had been wait some, and then wait some more, as the foursome ahead of Marion's group dragged its way around the course. Frustration became the mood of Heck and his playing partners, but they stuck it out.

Finally, at the 18th hole, a par-5, where the wait seemed even longer, the group in front hit their second shots. Marion and his friends then teed off. Driving their carts out to their shots they now waited in the fairway for the players ahead to leave the reachable green. *And then it happened.* One of the foursome from the 18th green got in a cart and started driving back to where Marion was standing in the middle of the fairway. "Now what?" said Marion under his breath.

When the cart pulled up the player asked Marion if his group had seen a putter left on the previous hole. Heck couldn't believe what the man was asking. "Could it be the one you are holding in your left hand?" he offered as a suggestion. Yes, the man had taken the putter out of his bag when he pulled his cart up to the 18th green. Then he apparently got distracted and looked for it again but didn't see it in the bag because it was in his left hand. He drove all the way back to Heck using his right hand to steer the cart, then popped the question that he probably wished he had never asked. He was looking in the wrong place asking the wrong people.

This Ought to Do the Trick

If you are ever in the British Isles and looking for an entertaining speaker, go no further than John Stirling, a British PGA member and national coach. In his wonderful Scottish dialect he relates an experience of his youth in the following fashion.

> As a lad I was poor as a church mouse. Working on the golf course at age 14 brought in a few shillings to share with the family but not enough to buy a second pair of shoes. The one pair I owned was starting to fall apart. The sole had come loose in the front of the right shoe and it would catch the ground if I didn't swing my leg up a bit as I walked. While cutting the green on the local course where I worked, I was pushing the mower while swinging my foot upward to clear the turf from my damaged shoe. A group of members approached the hole, so I pulled the mower off to the side. When the group got closer, I recognized one of the players as the richest man in the whole area. He'd hit his third shot onto the green.
>
> While the others were playing up, he came over to me and said, "Lad, what's wrong with yer foot?"

"It's not me foot, sir, it's me shoe." I said, raising my foot for him to see the hanging sole.

With that he reached in his pocket and pulled out a roll of money the size I'd never seen in my life. Hundred pound notes, even, so much that he needed a rubber band around the wad to hold it together. My heart started pounding in anticipation of a grand gift as he undid the roll. Then he handed me the rubber band he'd taken off and said, "Here, this might help."

THE MAGIC REMINDER

This may be one of those apocryphal tales that you are not quite sure about. It was told to me several years ago. An old pro had come from another state to teach at this public range as an independent contractor teacher. He would sit out in a chair watching players swing, waiting for anyone that sought him out for a lesson. There was a mysterious, almost metaphysical air about him, as he was so quiet and looked so wise. His teaching points were simple; he said little and watched a lot. Every once in awhile, after a student hit a shot, the pro would reach in his back pocket and pull out a folded-over piece of paper, glance at it, then return it to his pocket. Some of the juniors who hung around the range became curious about what magical information was written on the paper. They tried for days to get the right moment when they could slip it out of his pocket to discover the contents. Finally, three of them were able get him on the putting green in the pretense of showing them something. While he was bent over, one of the boys "accidentally" bumped him from behind and pulled out the paper. They couldn't wait to get together in the restroom to see what it said. When they unfolded it, the message was, "A slice goes to the right, a hook goes to the left." I guess it was just a reminder.

Not a Dangerous Group

It was an early West Virginia morning. By 7:40 a foursome had already finished the third hole at this mountain course even after having teed off in a heavy fog. The walk to the fourth tee was single file through a small stretch of woods. As they came out onto the tee, the sun was starting to burn through the fog and the day was improving. The hole was a lovely 167-yard par-3 where you hit from an elevated tee down to a target green surrounded by bunkers, pampas grass, and the ever-present trees. What was unusual about the upcoming shot was that the green was occupied not by golfers, but by five wild turkeys. It was Mother Nature in her full glory.

At first everyone was silent, just taking in this glorious sight. Then they started to talk about what they were going to hit and how the bets stood when one of the group made this observation. "Don't you guys think it's kind of strange that those birds haven't moved on the green? Usually they are pretty easily spooked, and they gotta be able to hear us up here yet don't seem concerned."

Listening to all this commentary, one of the caddies said, "Those birds—they're smarter than you think. They know when they're in danger and when they're not. And *they ain't in no danger getting hit by this group!*"

And Here's What I Think of Your Game

In the early 1920s an English member of the Royal and Ancient Golf Club of St. Andrews decided to come up from London to the "auld toun" a week early in preparation for the club championship. Although not a good player, he was hoping to make a decent showing in his flight, possibly even do well enough to move up to a lower one the following year. He hired a local caddy to take him around and help him with his game.

Starting the week in bad form, he began to improve after a couple of days, particularly with the help of the caddy's swing suggestions. Getting plenty of practice and an equal amount of encouragement from his caddy, his spirits were high as the opening round approached. The day before the start of the tournament the pairings were posted and he found that he was playing a Mr. J. McAndrew. That afternoon, he finished his final tune-up on the course. While receiving additional praise from his caddy on his progress, he asked about the game of a Mr. J. McAndrew.

"Ach," said the caddy. "He canna drive, canna pitch or putt, he is terrible. Why da ya ask?"

"Well," the member replied with a cherry tone, "That's who we're playing tomorrow."

"Ach, he'll beat ya," was the unexpected but apparently honest reply.

A caddy with an honest assessment.

Get the Player's Starting Time

In the early days of golf in Scotland the play was on public ground where a variety of activities could be going on at the same time. There might be people walking their dogs, laying out wash on the turf, children playing, or golfers golfing. If you have ever wondered why in the old days golfers wore red jackets, it was to warn people that golfers were in the area with the intent of helping to keep passersby from being hit with a ball.

There is a rather busy crossing place on the Old Course at St. Andrews right on the first and 18th fairways where people could go back and forth from the beach to town. One day at the first tee a member of the R & A played off, striking a man crossing the fairway, hitting him squarely in the head and causing him to fall to the ground. It turned out to be one of the caddies who was on his way from the caddy-waiting benches, quite likely to the pub. The member bent over the shabbily-dressed character who seemed to be either out cold or dead, and asked the man if he was okay. No response. Again he asked him; still no response. The member then slipped a gold sovereign coin into the fallen man's hand. Feeling the coin, the prostrate caddy slightly opened one eye, and now seeing the coin that he had before only felt, said, "And what time might you be coming out tomorrow, sir?"

Honestly, We Were Looking for a Ball

Meadowbrook Country Club just outside of Detroit, in Northville, Michigan, is a very enjoyable place to be a member. It has a tournament history, having hosted the PGA Tour Motor City Open for several years, employed several good professionals including PGA Hall of Famer Chick Harbert, and always presents a finely groomed member-playable course. It was a pleasure for me to serve there as an assistant one season in the summer of 1960. Supposedly this is a story that took place just before that time.

In Midwestern summers you can play golf up to about 9:30 p.m. In fact, starting late is a kind of treat when the day has been especially hot. One member couple decided to go out after dinner about 8:30 p.m. just to play a few holes. They lived nearby so drove to the course, grabbed a handful of clubs each, and headed out. It was getting dark when they reached the par-3 sixth hole, and they were a good distance away from the clubhouse. That hole is an uphill shot where it is difficult to see the bottom of the flagstick from the tee when its placement is near the back of the green. The sun had started to go down but there was just enough lingering light to make this their final hole. The husband hit a good-looking shot right at the flag, but with the fading light it was hard to tell if it was the right distance. His wife hit a poor tee shot and decided just to pick up. When they got near the green they didn't see the husband's ball so they looked over the back of the green, thinking he had hit it over. The rough was long. After a short hunt they were unable to locate the ball so decided to give up and just head for home. After a late night snack, a little TV, and some reading in bed, the light was turned out and they settled into a good night's sleep.

Momentarily, the husband bolted up in bed. "What's the matter?" questioned his wife.

"Did you look in the hole?" he asked.

"What are you talking about?" she responded.

"Did you look in the cup on the last hole we played to see if my ball was in there?"

"No, I didn't look in the cup," was her answer.

His head went back down on the pillow but only for a short time. He got up and went to the closet.

"What are you doing?" she asked as she turned on the light and saw him put on his bathrobe and slippers.

"I've got to go check to see if it's in the hole."

"Are you crazy? It's almost midnight!" said his exasperated wife.

But he was determined. It wasn't long before she heard the car pull out of the driveway. In just a few moments it pulled back in. He appeared at the bedroom door, flashlight in hand. "Now what?" she asked.

"I need a witness."

"You've got to be kidding!"

"Look," he said, "I have never had a hole-in-one. This may be my only chance."

Soon there were two people in their bathrobes pulling up to the totally empty parking lot near the clubhouse. They hiked across the pavement, past the clubhouse, across the grass and up to the sixth hole, the husband leading the way with the flashlight. Once they reached the green they headed straight for the flagstick, which was still in its place on the green, shined the light down into the cup, and...there was no ball. At that moment a night security guard pulled up in a golf cart. He shined his light on them, revealing their manner of dress, and said, "What are you people doing?"

The answer was an honest, "We are members, and we're just looking for a ball. Goodnight."

THE COUNTRY'S LEADER

If you have visited St. Andrews, you must have gone by the Royal and Ancient clubhouse, which stands just behind and to the side of the 18th green of the Old Course. The raised walk in back of the home hole gives any interested party the chance to view the players coming to the green, and in particular their putting when they reach it.

There was a larger-than-average gathering at that location on this particular day as the Prime Minister of Great Britain, Lord Balfour, was playing. By the time his party was putting, the crowd had swelled to watch their leader's stroke. He was about 40 feet from the cup and his caddy was giving him the correct line by holding the flagstick under his arm and then dipping it just above the surface of the green indicating that there was a two-foot break from right to left, so to aim that distance to the right. Prime Minister Balfour putted and the ball started two feet left rather than right and ended up further off the mark in that direction. The caddy stood there for a moment looking baffled by the result. Then he turned to the

The Prime Minister couldn't follow directions.

crowd and loudly announced, *"And these are the bloody bastards that are runnin' the country!"*

Observations and Quips

In a couple of pseudo golf studies, one conducted at M.I.T. showed that bad shots come in groups of three. If you hit a fourth bad shot it is the first of the next group of three. In another supposed "study" at Harvard on private golf clubs, the following was discovered. "Under the most vigorously-controlled conditions of pressure, temperature, volume, humidity, and other variables, it was found that a member of a country club will do what he damned well pleases."

John May, a former editor at *Golf Digest*, had a quick wit and whimsical sense of humor. While preparing to putt on the 18th green in a match at his club, John stopped. A nearby phone was ringing (this was long before cell phones made their appearance in our world) and the unmistakable sound was coming from his golf bag. He excused himself to the group, went over to the fringe, unzipped a side pocket, and took out a toy telephone. He held the phone to his ear for a moment, nodded his head, said thank you, and hung up. Then he turned to the others and announced, "God says it breaks seven inches to the right." It was a classic John May joke.

George Brett, Hall of Fame third baseman for the Kansas City Royals, was once asked during a round of golf how he was playing. "Three over," was his reply. "One over a house, one over a patio, and one over a swimming pool."

In a charity golf event where a car was being awarded on a par-3 hole, a high handicap player hit a 4-wood that struck the hood of the car parked behind the green. One of his playing partners said, "I don't think you understand. You get the car if you hit the hole, not the car."

Butch Baird, father of Tour player Briny Baird, was a steady competitor on the PGA Tour over a long period of time. As his career on the junior circuit was coming to a close and the Senior Tour was in sight, he was asked by a golf writer if he was planning to play on the Senior Tour. "Haven't really thought much about it," he said. "After all, it's still one year, two months, 18 days, four hours and 20 minutes away."

Milton Gross, author of *Eighteen Holes in My Head,* provides us with this brief verse that pretty much sums it up for the avid golfer.

> To all of us
> Who have ballmarks on our clubs
> Where they shouldn't be,
> Scars on our souls
> Only we can see,
> And chains on our wrists
> We can't get free.

Paul Harvey is a giant in the radio broadcast world—the most listened to news commentator ever. So it was a treat to be able to join him at his club, Bob O'Link, outside Chicago, for a game of golf along with the home professional Gary Groh, and Sunset Ridge professional Tom Wilcox. While we were getting ready to tee off Paul said, "Fellas, I talk to millions of people on the radio every day and to thousands of people in auditoriums when I give speeches. It doesn't bother me a bit. But standing on the first tee with three golf professionals, *my knees are shakin'.*"

QUOTES

"Your financial cost can best be figured out when you realize that if you were to devote the same time and energy to business instead of golf, you would be a millionaire in approximately six weeks." **Buddy Hackett**

"The last year's champion [at the Masters] serves as the host. He chooses the menu and picks up the tab. When I discovered the cost of the dinner was more than the prize money, I finished second four times." **Ben Hogan**

"Sam Snead's got more money buried underground in his backyard than I ever made on top. He's got gophers that subscribe to *Fortune* magazine." **Arnold Palmer**

"Corey Pavin is a little on the slight side. When he goes through a turnstile, nothing happens." **Jim Moriarty**

"I think all that rain shrunk the cups." **Juli Inkster** (after a poor putting round in the rain)

"I played so badly I got a get well card from the IRS." **Johnny Miller**

"My name used to be O'Connor but I changed it for business reasons." **Chi Chi Rodriguez**

"At first I said, 'Let's play for taxes.'" **Michael Jordan** (on playing with President Clinton for the first time)

"Variety may be the spice of life, but it's monotony that brings home the groceries." **Anonymous**

Golf Zaniness Around the World

It has been my good fortune to visit 32 countries in my career of teaching and playing golf. While some things in golf are the same no matter where you go (people slice in every country), there are other things that are quite different. Sometimes the differences bring to light unusual experiences. Though we don't cite examples for all 32 countries, many of the following vignettes do come from outside the USA.

THE BEST GOLF BARGAIN IN THE WORLD

If you stop at the famous Gullane Golf Club outside Edinburgh on the way to Muirfield you may be lucky enough to see Archie Baird on the course. Archie is the local golf historian and curator of the Gullane Golf Museum. Play with Archie and you will either be carrying your clubs or pulling a trolley, but for certain you *will* be playing fast. One other thing, Archie's dog will be right along with you. To include your dog while walking the course is quite acceptable in Scotland, and in my view, a very civilized idea at that. Archie is one of the golf collecting world's more passionate members. He says his greatest claim to fame in that hobby is his wife, Sheila. She was a Park, granddaughter of Open winner, club maker, and course designer Willie Park Jr. and great granddaughter of Willie Park Sr., who became the first Open Champion in 1860. Because of that, Shelia Park Baird has earned from Archie the title, "The Ultimate Collectible."

Although we played the fine Gullane course together, Archie told me that he was going to give me a special treat. We were going to play one of the world's most famous, or at least formerly famous, golf venues—the old nine-hole racetrack Mussleburgh Links. It is right next to the highway as you are heading to North Berwick, Muirfield and Gullane, but at the time you would have to look closely to identify it as a place where anybody played the game now or ever. We drove into a patchy grass and dirt parking lot where a cement hut stood that gave an indication it was a starter's booth, but no one was home. In fact *no* one was in sight on the entire course, which jumped its way over and back across a racetrack that, like the golf course, had seen better times. Yet, if you have read the golf history books you realize we were about to step onto hallowed ground. These same holes were played by the Dunn brothers of Mussleburgh against "Old and Young" Tom Morris of St. Andrews in the 1860s for £400 a side, a fortune in those days. The man considered to be the first true golf professional, Allan Robertson, played here, as did many more champions, including the Parks, since this course was a venue for not only challenge matches but also for the Open.

A primitive marker on the ground indicated the teeing area for the first hole, which featured a small undulating green some 340 yards distant. After playing our tee shots over the racetrack, we soon reached the putting surface that would challenge the greatest putters of today, partly because of its slope, but more because of its condition. The flagstick turned out to be a rod of iron, about four feet high, with a rag tied around the top. It wasn't Winged Foot, but it was golf. Archie and I enjoyed the fellowship and the sharing of stories about the famous players of the 1800s as we toured the rolling, sparsely turf-covered fairways. Then came a highlight. As we came to the eighth tee I saw the house known as Mrs. Forman's. I distinctly remember having read about how she served drinks to the golfers through the pass-through window on the side of her stark gray home. Situated at the eighth hole, it was sort of a "not quite halfway house." That was 150 years ago! Now here it was, only a few yards away. While viewing it, all the names from the past that she must have served flooded my mind: Park, Dunn, Morris, Fernie, Robertson, Kirk, Ferguson, Brown, Strath, Hunter, Smith, Martin, those players who were the predecessors to the "Great Triumvirate" of Vardon, Braid, and Taylor, men we consider to be so early in golf. It was a magical moment, but not the highlight of the day. That awaited us on the ninth fairway.

The home hole, number nine, is a par-5, meandering back toward the car park and starter's hut. We had played our drives and were walking down the fairway when a tall, elderly man approached us. He was wearing a long overcoat along with the traditional flat Scottish woolen hat. He carried a clear plastic sack that contained a roll of tickets. With no form of introduction he simply said, "I'll be havin' yer green fee." It was evident there would be no free golf today. When I inquired as to the amount, he said, "That'll be two shillings each." What did I hear? Was I being told that to play one of the historically most significant golf courses in the world I would be paying 24 cents! Was this a dream or a time warp to another century? It turns out neither, just Scotland offering the best buy in the game.

Note: It is my understanding that the Mussleburgh Links course has been refurbished and now is a gem.

It's All in the Name

The Stan Thompson Golf Company out of California made quality equipment, especially custom woods. Stan himself was a most likeable business leader with a small but successful company. You may recall a big seller of theirs, "The Ginty." It was one of the first modern clubs to utilize a rail effect on the bottom of a fairway wood. This feature lowered the center of gravity and made it easy to get the ball up in the air, particularly when playing out of the rough.

The inspiration for the club came from Stan himself. After a day on the course in which he had trouble escaping from the rough, he hit upon an idea that came from his experience as a sailor. Stan spent as much time with his sailboat as he did on the golf course. When his drives found the rough and the fairway wood he was using couldn't cut through the grass, he thought about how the keel of his boat cuts through the water. If he could design a club with a keel-like effect, maybe it would do in grass what his boat keel did in water. So he had one of his plant employees slug some lead onto the bottom of a lofted fairway wood, shaped it like a keel, and took it out for a test. He was amazed at how effective it was in both cutting through the grass and getting the ball up in the air. After some refining of his first attempt, but leaving it still in a rough stage, he called in his two national sales managers. One was from east of the Mississippi and the other from the west. He told them he had a new product for them to try. They looked at the prototype but were unimpressed by what they saw. When they returned from trying it out, however, their opinions had changed. It was obvious this was going to be a winner. Excitedly they asked Stan, "What are you going to call the club?"

Realizing that it didn't look pretty. Stan replied, "Ginty."

Misunderstanding what Stan said, the Eastern manager said,

"Stan, you can't call it that. We have a whole bunch of Italian pros in the East, and 'guinea' is a derogatory name to them."

"I didn't say 'guinea,'" replied Stan, "I said, Ginty!"

"What is a Ginty?" both of them inquired.

"A ginty is the smallest, homeliest runt in a Scottish family," explained Stan. And that is what they called it (Stan would have known, he was a pure Scot).

Now That's Efficient

The sound was unmistakable. I had heard it too many times in my career. It was the clicking of rubber tees on a golf driving mat and the crack of a golf ball being driven. I was being awakened by this sound at 7 a.m. while lying in my bed on the 11th floor of a hotel in Osaka, Japan. But how was this possible? Buildings surrounded us, no driving range was in sight, and only a baseball park across the street broke up the very commercial look of the neighborhood. I got up and looked out the window. It was the ballpark.

Starting near first base on the right field side of the diamond above the stands was an additional two stories of driving range cubicles, and they were beginning to fill up. It was then that I noticed beyond the wall in the outfield there arose a high netting that kept the balls inside the all-dirt ballpark. By the time my wife and I returned from breakfast the ball diamond began to resemble a large brown cookie with tiny white sprinkles covering its top.

After we attended a couple of meetings at the hotel, we returned to our room to prepare our things for an afternoon demonstration/clinic nearby. I looked out the window again, just in time to see a large net roll down across the front of the range bays. At that moment two trucks drove onto the field from a gate in the right-field foul area. Following the trucks were about 20 workers, some carrying a piece of equipment resembling a push broom but with a flat wooden board in place of the bristles; and others carried scoop shovels. The crew was out there to pick up the balls. The balls were pushed by the "brooms" into piles, scooped up by the shovels, and tossed into the dump trucks. When the field had been cleared, the dump trunks drove over to an area halfway down the right-field line near the stands. There a large covered door opened from the ground, exposing a chute into which the dump trucks delivered the balls. They would then be carried on a conveyor, through a wash cycle and back up to the dispensing machines on the range.

When the workers and trucks left the field at about 11 a.m., a crew came out to lay the lines on the diamond and prepare the field for the double header that was to start at 12:30. Not long after, the teams came out for pregame practice and we left for our demonstration. When we returned to our room at 6:00 p.m., the second game was just finishing. As soon as it was over, the net covering the hitting bays went up, the lights went on, and the same sound that woke me up that morning started all over again.

Raking up the golf balls before the next baseball game.

EXPERIENCES IN NORTHERN SCOTLAND

Before the advent of Golf Digest schools in the United States and the proliferation since, the Scots had their own version in the northern part of their country. It was called the Nairn Golf Week, held at the Nairn Golf Club on the Firth of Moray. I was the first American ever invited to join the teaching staff and looked forward to that experience. My wife, Ione, accompanied me and so was present when we checked in at the lovely old hotel that had once been the Earl of Moray's private estate. The first words we heard from any staff was from the hall porter who was bringing in our luggage. "Ya know what Nairn stands for?" he asked. We didn't, so he gave us his stock reply, "Na rain, Na rain." That wasn't true because we had our share of rain that week, but the Scots didn't seem to mind.

The teaching staff was marvelous. Heading up the group was Dai Rees, three-time British Open runner-up and 10 times a member of the Ryder Cup team, including six captaincies. He was a delightful character, full of energy and fun. Dai was undoubtedly the main reason that the Nairn Golf Week had succeeded for so many years. Also on the staff was Harry Bannerman, a young Ryder Cup player from Aberdeen; Jesse Valentine, one of Britain's most celebrated female golfers; Jimmy Wilson, a veteran teacher from Pitlochary in central Scotland; and Gregor McIntosh, the Nairn professional.

The school was very informal and relaxed in its conduct. Players would show up in the morning after breakfast for a short lecture, followed by some practical demonstration, then out to the range—or practice pitch as they call it—where each teacher had a full swing station. The players would cue up in a line behind the tee area of the pro from whom they wished to get help. After a few choice tips they would pull their trollies over to the first tee and play off. Teachers would then join them during the round. The irony came when I was extolling the then-popular

"American style" of "drive the legs, pull through with the left side," while not 10 yards away Gregor McIntosh would be saying, "Low back, keep yer eye on the ball, and hit the hell out of it with yer right hand." Under the windy conditions they faced every day, Gregor was right.

Proof of that came when they had a long drive exhibition that turned out also to be a lesson…for me. Having won a few long drive contests in my career and sizing up the opposition, I looked forward to the challenge when I noted it on the schedule. On the day of the event we got a taste of real Scottish wind. A gale was blowing off the water directly into the face of the long drive contestants. As I prepared to hit I tried to picture the 300-plus-yard drives I had just rattled off at St. Andrews a few days before. Each contestant received three balls. After I hit my third ball toward the Firth with my "American style" swing, the longest was measured at 197 yards. "Low back, keep yer eye on the ball, and hit the hell out of it with yer right hand," won at 212.

Before leaving the story of Nairn I am reminded of the irascible Max Faulker, Open Champion of Great Britain in 1951, who was once asked by a student at the golf school what the great Faulker thought of the student's driver. Max said, "If I were you I would immediately walk down to the beach, get close to the water, wind up and making your strongest swing, let go of the club, drowning it in the Firth, *never to be seen again.*"

CHECKING FOR CALLUSES

Shinjuku Station in Tokyo is the busiest train station in the world. I was standing on the platform waiting for the "Bullet Train" to Osaka, but I was not alone. Accompanying me was my wife, an interpreter, a huge amount of luggage, and three Japanese golf teaching professionals who had been conscripted to haul all of our things from the vans through the huge terminal building and down to the platform. There was no sign of the train that was due in about six minutes, but we knew it would arrive right on the dot. That is the way the train system operates in Japan.

While standing there the interpreter said, "Excuse me, Dr. Wiren, but the professionals want to know if you can look at their hands to see if their calluses are in the right place for a good golfer."

"Certainly," I replied and started my inspection as they offered their hands forward. I was stunned! Only on the hands of the most seasoned common laborer had I ever seen palms with so much callous buildup. These pros must have hit thousands of balls, and their calluses were in exactly the right spots. There was a pause before the interpreter asked me if I would allow the pros to check my calluses. I held out both my hands that were as smooth as a baby's skin.

There erupted a staccato of Japanese remarks as the astonished men examined them. Their commentary caused the interpreter to laugh. "What did they say?" I questioned.

Again he laughed and then explained, "They said, 'Wiren-san must have a secret!'"

THE DREAM

It was to be the first of several trips I made to Australia, but this one seemed extra special. When you are going somewhere for the first time there is always a bit more anticipation, in this case, even some anxiety. After all, Australia is such a grand sporting country, one that has produced more than its share of great golfers, from Peter Thomson to Greg Norman and a host of others in between. On this initial visit I wanted to perform well during my scheduled clinic/exhibitions and to make a favorable impression. However, two weeks before our departure, apparently I slept in a wrong position one night and woke up the next day with a neck that was definitely not aligned correctly. Over the years I had experienced recurring neck problems, a result of too many head-on tackles while playing linebacker for four years in college football. My customary therapy then was to visit the local chiropractor the day after a game to get "an adjustment." The "cure" was usually fairly swift, so I could experience good range of motion again within a day or two of the treatment, sometimes even sooner. But this time it didn't work. In fact it seemed to get worse. At the golf course my drives were anemic, slicing into the woods at about 240 yards. My left arm seemed numb so I couldn't generate any speed. This was very disturbing because my scheduled clinics always featured shot demonstrations with the highlight "end of the show" 300-yard drive.

That was about the time when the dreams began. I have read dream books with the explanation that many of the things you dream about have a direct relationship to what is currently going on in your life, even if the images and incidents are sometimes incongruous. My dream wasn't strange at all, and it repeated itself three times over the next week, holding no subtle or hidden meanings. It was about as obvious as one could get: performance anxiety.

In the dream I am standing on the first tee at a tournament paired in a threesome with Sam Snead and Jack Nicklaus. There is a huge crowd around us that has pushed in so close that there was just enough room to make a golf swing. In fact, I thought the guy standing right behind us smoking the cigar would get it knocked out of his mouth when Sam, the first to hit, took his backswing. The crowd urged Sam to hit one of his "big drives," so "The Slammer" reached back and pumped one out there about 275 yards. Now it was "The Golden Bear's" turn. Again, encouraged by the gallery to really smash one, Jack stretched high into his backswing and drilled a huge slightly fading ball to the 290 yard mark—a real boomer. I was next.

Right around the time of the dreams I actually had been competing in some local long drive contests with good success, so it was logical that the fans were egging me on to show these great players a really long one. I reached for my driver (wooden headed at the time) and pulled off the woolen head cover that had a large decorative pom-pom on the end of it. When I got the cover off I stared at my driver in disbelief. It looked as though it recently had been lacquered so that it was still very tacky, and it had all kinds of fuzzy strings attached to it from the head cover. I tried some practice swings that made a "whooshing" sound, but the added resistance from the fuzzy material wouldn't allow me to generate any speed. I swung repeatedly until the crowd lost patience and started to shout, "C'mon, hit the ball."

My response was, "I can't get any speed…I can't get any speed." And that was where the dream ended…frustration and obvious trepidation about my upcoming trip. Relief for my neck came the day before leaving. The trip was great, the show highlight drives went 300 yards, and I developed a greater appreciation for the veracity of the dream world.

SECURITY…JOB OR NO JOB

Andra Kirkaldy was the honorary professional at the Royal and Ancient Golf Club from 1910 to 1934. Andra was a large man who was as strong as he was big. He once demonstrated that fact during a match where a spectator was harassing him. He had hit his ball into the "burn" (a small creek) that runs just in front of the first green of the Old Course. Apparently the man had made a wager on Andra and was chiding him for the poor shot. Andra picked him up by the "brechts" (the pants) and held him at arm's length over the burn until the man pleaded for mercy.

Kirkaldy was a fine player but his personality, one might say was, "rough a-round the edges." I heard that his schooling came from the streets and the links, so that he never learned to read. He could be seen sitting at times on a bench outside the clubhouse holding a newspaper, albeit upside down. His hard manner once caused the captain of the club to have a serious talk with Kirkaldy. "Andra," he said, "Ya got to be changin' yer way. Yer ta rough with the members. Ya need ta act nicer to them.

Andra Kirkaldy felt secure.

If ya don't man, ya kin lose yer job. Ya'll be outta werk, na money to buy food."

"Ach," said Andra, seemingly unperturbed about that possibility, *"I'm sleepin' with every cook in toun."*

Thanks for the Advice!

Jerry Cowman, of Sioux Falls, South Dakota, once told me of a time when he and his wife worked a tournament at the local Elmwood Park Course. It was a charity event that offered a special prize of a new Cadillac for a hole-in-one. Their job was to monitor the hole and serve as witnesses. They were stationed alongside the tee box as the golfers came through. Several groups had passed without there being a winner, when along came "Bucky" and his foursome. Bucky was competitive and he had an eye on that car. As they waited for the group on the green to finish Bucky kind of moseyed over to Jerry and asked, "What's everybody hitting from here?"

"Mostly 4-irons," Jerry said.

"Hey, thanks."

"No problem."

Bucky teed it up, took three practice swings, and hit the prettiest 4-iron shot you'd ever want to see, right at the flagstick, but about six feet short of the green. "Hey, I thought you said everybody was hitting 4-irons here."

"They are," Jerry said, "And they're all coming up about six feet short…you should have hit a 3-iron."

Cowman concluded, "I think if my wife hadn't been with me…well, who knows."

Just Need to Get a Few Things Right

Willie Park Jr. was a very dour Scot, not one for lighthearted repartee, especially when it came to learning golf. While giving a lesson to a noted barrister in Mussleburgh, his student became frustrated over having been told of some additional "principles" in the swing to which he would have to attend. "For God's sake,

Park," he bellowed, "Every time I come there's more to learn about the swing. How many bloody things are there?"

Without hesitation, Park, the former medical student who knew his anatomy and human movement said, *"As nearly as I can figure, there are 1,324!"*

Doesn't One Size Fit All?

Thanks to Dr. George McDonald I know about the teenage girl who worked for a dentist in Worthington, Minnesota. She wanted to have her dad buy her a car. The dentist knew that her dad loved to play golf, so he offered the young girl some golf balls she could give her dad as a present to soften him up. They were a *Spalding XL* brand. She thanked him for the gift but then looked at him rather puzzled. The dentist asked if there was a problem, and she said, "Are you sure that these are his size?"

It Is Important in Some Places to Look Good

During the two-plus decades that I traveled to Japan to teach, play, and give seminars, I devoted much of my time to presenting exhibition clinics at driving ranges where we held our Mizuno Golf Schools. On one occasion my group, which usually consisted of an interpreter, photographer, agent, and a couple of staff people from International Golf Research, arrived at this large range that was located in the heart of an industrial complex a couple of hours outside of Tokyo. The usual American and Japanese flags flew outside and some large welcome signs in both English and Japanese added festive appeal for the soon-to-arrive audience. When we drove up, there was the customary greeting by the course officials and the usual ushering us to a private

Welcome Dr. Gary Wiren

After the performance, waiting for the chauffeur.

room where tea and cookies were on the table along with miniature flags of our two countries. A short period of greeting and conversation was always the polite way of introducing one another before beginning any business transaction, meeting, or performance.

After our brief socializing, it was time to go outside, prepare our equipment, and warm up. The range was closed for the exhibition, so we were hitting out in the grass. The 150 chairs that partially surrounded the demo area were soon filled with an audience. The crowd was receptive to the jokes, stunts, and shots. We had an enjoyable hour together and I finished off with my closer, the 300-yard drive. I didn't always "pure it" in these performances, but on this occasion it was perfect.

As we packed up and were putting our things away in a large Toyota luxury car provided by the range owner, he came out to give me a beautifully wrapped present. He was not a typical looking Japanese, as he had a goatee and Fu Manchu style mustache that made him resemble an elderly Chinese philosopher. It turns out Mr. Suzuki was not only the owner of the driving range, but also of a good part of the industry that surrounded it. The range was his toy. When I accepted the gift with the customary bow, his white-gloved chauffeur who was driving us back opened the trunk of this black sedan to put in the gift. The trunk was spotless, and contained only one visible item, a brand new set of the very most expensive golf clubs encased in a gorgeous bag.

"My, that's a great set of clubs," I said through my interpreter. "What is Suzuki-san's handicap?"

The answer was a classic. "Oh, I don't play golf. They just look good in the trunk." (You think golf isn't important in Japan?)

THAT'S MY JOB DESCRIPTION

The most refreshing characteristic of the old Scot caddy is his absolute candor. They call them the way they see them. An American was excited about playing the Old Course at St. Andrews but found the drive to the ancient town was taking longer from Edinburgh than he thought. As usual, it was because of traffic on the Firth of Forth Bridge. He was lucky to locate a parking spot close by, rushed with his clubs to the first tee, and found that his group was up next. Trying to get ready, what with paying his fee and securing his caddy, he realized he had left his golf shoes in the car. He pulled his keys out of the golf bag, handed them to the caddy, and indicated where the car was parked, telling him to bring the shoes that were on the front seat. Handing back the keys, the caddy looked at him, and said, "I'm paid to carry, not to fetch and carry."

There's No Place Like Home

Ask the golf professionals in Michigan who was the best senior player in that state for several years and they will say Larry Mancour. He won the Michigan Open (not Seniors) on the difficult Bear Course in Traverse City when he was 52 years old. Larry found some time between winning events to tell me of an overseas adventure:

> A bunch of us went to Ireland and Scotland to play. It was my first time over. We played several of the most famous courses in Ireland first. Then we went to Scotland and experienced Troon and the Old Course at St. Andrews. One of my favorite courses in Scotland was Western Gailes. We played there early in the morning on a blustery, rainy day. After the round we went into the clubhouse to dry off, go to the restroom, and have a drink. While inside I ran into this old-time member who was probably in his 80s. He noticed that I was wet after being on the course and said, "Well, laddie, how'd ya find the course?"
>
> Since it was one of the best ones we had played at that time, I said, "This is a fine golf course."
>
> He answered, "It's the best."
>
> "Yes it is good." Then I named some of the other courses we had played: Troon, Royal Country Down, Turnberry, and St. Andrews.
>
> He said, "Yeah, laddie, this is the best."
>
> I changed tactics with the old gentleman. "It is a pretty old course."
>
> He replied, "My father was one of the founders of this

course. My father played here all of his life, and I have played here all of my life, and this is the best."

"I've got to pretty much agree with you, but we've played some other good courses, several in this area. Do you play all of them yourself?"

He said, "Laddie, I've never played another golf course. This is the best, so this is the only course I'll play."

THE SEMI-DROP

During one of the famous "between nines lunches" at a Japanese course this funny incident was brought to my attention. A group of college kids was out for their first time on the course. It was a cold day, and one of the players was wearing a pullover sweatshirt with a hood hanging in the back. On the eighth hole he sliced his drive into a water hazard. He walked down the steep bank on the edge of the water to look for his ball but had no success. Being schooled well in the rules before ever coming to the course, he took another ball, faced the hole and dropped his ball over his shoulder, as was the custom before the current arm's length rule. After the drop he turned and looked for the ball. To his surprise it wasn't there. Apparently it had bounced off the bank and directly into the water. So more carefully this time, he dropped another one, located it, and finished the hole. While he was sitting at lunch, a fellow student came by his seat and said, "What's this?" as she picked a ball out of the hood of his sweatshirt. It was his first drop that had never reached the ground.

Just Sharing the Duties

While serving as a consultant coach to the Italian Golf Federation and working with their national teams, I had a young golf professional share this experience with me. He had just finished his teacher training courses and was working at a good club that employed a very respected veteran teacher and player. A female club member had booked a playing lesson with the head pro, but he was called away. The pro asked the young assistant to take his place. The woman, who had been through some beginning lessons, was now looking for a lesson on the course so she could get a better feeling for the game. The assistant was as nervous as she after explaining he was a substitute, but he managed to do a decent job taking her around for four holes. He had several balls in a bag so that when she played a shot from the fairway and the result provided an opportunity for corrective instruction, he would do so by having her hit some more. When they left that spot he told her that he would retrieve the balls and she could take care of the divots. When they finished he felt satisfied that his first time out was a reasonable success. As he congratulated her and encouraged her to continue, she interrupted him and asked, "What do you want me to do with these?" She then unzipped the side pocket of her bag on the trolley and hauled out a large handful of divots.

Is This Really Golf in Germany?

Part of my philosophy related to golf is that whenever we get together in the name of golf we ought to be having a good time. So I try to punctuate my lessons and lectures with some fun. For example, in speaking to a group I have used this to serve that purpose. "How many of you have played golf in Scotland?"

usually a fair number of hands go up. "How about in Europe?" Now the number decreases. "Now, how many have played golf in Germany?" Usually, no hands are now in the air. "You know," I say, "Since Bernard Langer came to the forefront in professional golf, the game has become much more popular in Germany. But with golf being a relatively new sport in that country, the Germans have developed some words of their own to fit the game. Those of you who have studied the German language are familiar with the fact that it is not uncommon in their language to use extended long words that would be equivalent to multiple words in English. It's the same with their golf terms. For example, instead of our two words we use to identify a "golf course," the Germans use a single long word, *"hitundhuntenfield."* The word for a golfer is *"hitundhuntenfieldshvyippenshtickshvinger."* But the clubhouse is the best. They call it a *"hitundhuntenfieldshvyippenshtickshvingerstartundstopenplacedrinkinschpot."* (Some people don't believe me.)

Could I be explaining German golf terminology?

THE WRONG BALL

It was after the lunch rest period at the PGA National Golf Academy for Juniors, a summer golf camp for 12 to 18 year olds. I was serving as camp director. The young golfers had come from all over the world to the camp that was conducted at St. Andrews private school in Boca Raton, Florida, with the golf played at Boca West Golf Club, a nearby 54-hole venue. My daughter, Paige, and one of the campers, a sweet young girl from St. Louis named Stacy, were chatting in the girl's dorm. Paige, a recent high school graduate, had come down to assist me with some of the menial but necessary details like carrying water, putting equipment away, and generally cleaning up after activities. The previous school year, Paige had accepted the invitation to be a Palm Beach debutante. Ordinarily that was not our family's style. We lived in a nice but modest neighborhood, drove two used vehicles, and with raising four children had to watch the dollars. This invitation offered an experience that, while interesting, was going to be expensive, but Paige would have this chance only one time, so we agreed. Paige then went through the lengthy process of training and attending social events that culminated in a grand coming-out ball at the famous Breakers Hotel in Palm Beach.

Her golf camp dorm conversation partner, Stacy, had long blond hair, lovely large blue eyes, and seemed to be dreamily in awe or surprised about most everything. The two covered the usual topics that young teenage girls discuss until Paige innocently asked Stacy if they had a debutante ball in St. Louis.

"No," said Stacy, sounding puzzled, "But we do have the new Pinnacle," referring to Titleist's latest (at that time) golf product. In this case, it was the wrong ball.

How Thistle Dhu Got Its Name

For about nine years I wrote a complimentary quarterly news-letter that I sent to about 150 people in the golf world. I named it "Thistle Dhu." I'll never forget that Joe Dey, USGA Executive Director and later commissioner of the PGA Tour, once told me that it was something he always looked forward to receiving. I wrote it because I had started to develop a nice library of anti-quarian golf books and in reading them began to run across special anecdotes, observations, poems, and stories. I found myself wanting to share these with my golfing friends. Because the books were out-of-print and hard to come by, I was pretty certain that my recipients would never experience them other-wise. How the publication got its name is an interesting story.

During the 1920s there was a human migration that took place on the East Coast of our country that was not unlike birds who take flight to change their seasonal habitats. For many of the rich and famous it looked something like this: Newport Beach, the Hamptons, or Maine in the summer; Pinehurst in the fall; Palm Beach in the winter; and Pinehurst again in the spring on the way back to their summer hideaways. One such cyclical trav-eler was James Barber, who owned a passenger steamship line out of Boston and a large estate in Pinehurst. During one of the seasonal stops he had the usual houseful of guests. After their day of golf they were back at the estate but there was desire for some more play. The thought of going through the hassle of riding up to the club, getting equipment out, hiring caddies, etc. caused them to lose interest. This moment of unfulfilled desire gave Barber an idea. Why not build a miniature course on the property for the entertainment of his guests. To handle the task he hired Mr. E. H. Wiswell, an amateur architect with a creative if not devilish bent. Wiswell was to start work immedi-ately and have it ready for the return in the spring.

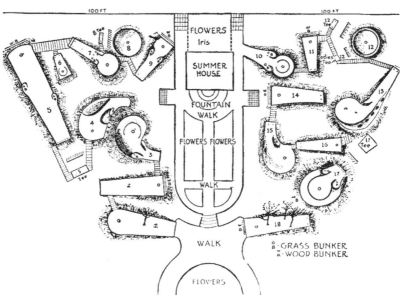

James Barber's Thistle Dhu course

When Barber returned the following season he and Wiswell toured the new layout together. The story has it that a guest followed along behind and overheard their conversation, including a comment from Barber, that it wasn't quite what he had in mind but "this'll do." Thinking the words were spoken to mean the name of the course, the guest translated it to "Thistle Dhu." It is considered to be the first miniature golf course in America. Courses of this type later came to be known as "Tom Thumb" courses. That name came from the famous midget in the Ringling Brothers Circus. But Barber's Thistle Dhu course was a private enterprise, and it took a few years for this early model to spin off a whole golf movement. That movement became a literal explosion of courses all over the country. In the late 1920s and early '30s it was hard to find a town of any size that didn't have a miniature golf putting course.

Late one evening, after I had finished volume one, number one of my new historical golf newsletter, I shut off the light in the study feeling I had created a brilliant piece of writing. I was taken aback the next morning to discover how my genius for concocting a literary gem had seemingly deteriorated while I slept. On rereading my maiden effort, I was now quite sure a Pulitzer wasn't in the wings. It was hardly the quality work I had envisioned the previous night, but...but...and that's when it came to me...it's not great, but, *this will do*. Knowing the Pinehurst story, I titled the newsletter "Thistle Dhu." And it did.

About Anything Goes in Skin City

Jack Sheehan is a personable plus handicap golfer who writes as well as he plays, maybe better. He has been covering the Las Vegas scene for over 20 years, which has been quite an eye-opener for him, having come from Hayden Lake, Washington, via the University of Oregon. With five books under his belt (his latest, *Skin City*, is a real blockbuster), he knows not only how to drop his putts but also how to drop some great lines on paper. Here is a glance at Las Vegas style hustler golf from Jack.

If you want to talk about some *real* money changing hands on the golf course in Vegas, you have to peel behind the television towers and the leader boards, back where IRS agents, manufacturing reps, and sportswriters are forbidden. You must venture to the land of the looping swing, the steel nerves, and the sharp pencil. Far removed from the public eye, in the crooked shadows of the Joshua trees, where the cicadas scream their mating song from the branches of oleanders…that's where they play for money that'll stop your heart.

One Vegas tournament that developed its own mythology was known as the Professionals Gamblers Invitational (PGI) and, believe me, Tiger and Ernie and Retief would not have been inclined to tee it up with those boys. As Doyle (Dolly) Brunson, a two-time winner of the World Series of Poker…says, "The pros on Tour certainly know about pressure but it's a different kind of stress. They're always playing for somebody else's money. See, when David Duval hits a putt for a 'hunnerd and fitty thousands,' he don't have to reach into his Dockers and come up with the cash if he misses it. We do."

Amarillo Slim, who has been a railbird at several Professional Gamblers events, says the gamblers tournament had a way of separating the men from the boys. "Some guys roar like a forest fire in their hometown," he says, "but when they come to Vegas and put up the big money, so much dog come out in 'em they could catch every possum in Louisiana."

The tournament director of the PGI for years was Jack Binion, part owner of Binion's Horseshoe Casino. The tournament started in 1974 as a way for Binion and Dolly Bunson to keep their poker friends in town for the summer. The format was match play, and the minimum bet was $500 Nassau, but as Binion said, "The base fee in the little gathering is just spare change; stuff to mark your ball with. We want guys who like to juice it a little. It's not uncommon to see a guy drop a hundred grand or more in a match!"

You could never find a lot of USGA rule books floating around the PGI. According to Binion, common sense is the best guide to settling gambling disputes. "The 14-club rule is ridiculous," Binion said, "so we let 'em take as many weapons as they wanted. And the stupidest rule ever is that a guy can't putt between his legs. We allowed almost any putting style. One time a guy got down and used the grip end of his putter as a cue stick. As I recall, we outlawed that. We don't really care how a guy does it as long as it vaguely resembles a golf stroke." Players need not bother inquiring about a free drop, no matter where their ball came to rest. "We always played it where it lay," Binion said. "Even cart paths and sprinklers and outhouses. Made for some fun shots."

In the PGI and other big games around Vegas, grease is usually allowed on the clubface. A little slippery elm, or K-Y Jelly, or Vaseline, balms that are normally applied while participating in more nocturnal games, can go a long way toward straightening out a nasty hook or runaway slice. Grease also increases distance off the tee as filled grooves diminish backspin on a ball, thereby increasing carry and roll.

The grease rule can inspire some live post-round conversation. "On 14 I had about 167 into a zephyr with a furry lie," said one participant spread over a corner booth at the bar of Las Vegas Country Club. "I'm thinking I'll hit a dry 6-iron and try to keep 'er low. Then the wind stops, so I decide to hit a moist eight and let that puppy hunt…Course I hit it fat. Took me 10 minutes to scrape the mud off."

Binion said the most he ever saw lost in a PGI match was $312,000. "The guy who dumped it couldn't break 90," he said. "But then, the guy who won the money couldn't either."

WHEN CADDIES KNOW BEST

Becoming the captain of the Royal and Ancient Golf Club of St. Andrews is quite an honor that deserves a ceremony to commemorate it. So appropriately there is just such an event, "the playing-in of the captain." The ceremony is accompanied by the

Quite a galley for one shot. Clapping is Willie Auchterlonie.

shooting of a small cannon along with the new captain striking a tee shot down the first fairway where the local caddies are gathered in an attempt to recover the ball. There is a gold sovereign prize given for the most adroit caddie that is successful in chasing it down, so you can imagine that competition is keen. In the picture from 1936 you see Willie Auchterlonie, Open Champion of 1893 who served for many years as the honorary professional to the Royal and Ancient Golf Club, standing on the left leading the applause. Playing himself in is Sir John Simons, who appears to have made contact, although his follow-through is somewhat suspect. The story is told of the time when the Prince of Wales was selected for the captaincy. As he prepared to play his tee shot, the caddies, desiring the piece of gold, stood "unflatteringly close to the teeing ground." Apparently they knew the Prince's game.

THE ORIGIN OF GOLF

Tracing the origin of the game of golf is not a simple visit to Scotland in the 1400s. Yes, St. Andrews University was founded in 1409 and it was noted that students were playing the game. It also is true that the Dutch had a similar game, even using the name of colf and kolf before this time. Furthermore, other countries in Europe had stick and ball sports that most likely came from the Roman game of paganica or paganicus that was introduced to them during the Roman occupation. But how about taking a step even further back? General Ho Ying-chin, honorary chairman of the Nationalist Chinese Golf Association, in the 1960s told an audience at a new golf course that Chinese warlords invented golf around 400-22 B.C. and called it "the ball hitting game."

Certainly the picture lends credibility to a golf-like game.

SO YOU THINK YOU KNOW YOUR OPENS

One of the great contributors to golf in the New England states has been Dick Haskell, former Executive Director of the Massachusetts Golf Association. He loved golf, he loved people, and he loved to have a good time. One of the fun things he did was to create a quiz that tested one's knowledge of past U.S. Open winners, both men and women. With his permission I have selected portions of those quizzes, made some additions to each, and developed a similar quiz for British Open winners. Enjoy!

Here is a sample to help you get the idea. The clue can pertain to either the first or last name of the particular winner. Then test your knowledge. The answers are at the end. Remember, either first or last names.

Sample:
1. Door lock............................answer... Tommy Bolt
2. Negative personality trait..........answer... Orville Moody
3. Big risk insurance company.......answer... Lloyd Mangrum
(Lloyd's of London)

The Open (British) Winner

1. Not a member of the clergy. He would be a _____.

2. Invaders of Britain: _____.

3. Material for a summer garment: _____.

4. Bird's beak: _____.

5. Clint Eastwood's "Dirty _____.

6. Buildings on a farm: _____.

7. New York stage award: _____.

8. Custom clothing fitter and maker: _____.

9. A food tradesman and bird (hyphenated): _____.

10. Famous British newspaper: _____ *Mail.*

11. Makeup of DNA and splicing: _____.

12. A male athlete's protection device: _____.

U.S. Men's Open Winners

1. Man who grinds wheat for bread: _____.

2. (Italian) Wine for three: _____.

3. "Et tu, Brute": _____.

4. Blue and yellow: _____.

5. Size comparison: _____.

6. Goose liver: _____.

7. Frozen rain: _____.

8. Admiral Byrd discovery: _____.

9. Holmes' sidekick: _____.

10. Scottish kings of similar name: _____.

11. Medieval fighting regalia: _____.

12. This person was a "good man": _____.

U.S. WOMEN'S OPEN WINNERS

1. Think of wolves and cards: _____.

2. *Little Women* author: _____.

3. Robert Louis: _____.

4. A Christmas song: _____.

5. Disney World character: _____.

6. Children's book, *Charlotte's:* _____.

7. Downed the *Titanic*: _____.

8. Term for infant: _____.

9. Most critical piece in chess: _____.

10. Cantaloupe and honeydew: _____.

11. Salt and: _____.

12. Last name rhymes with Tracy: _____.

Answers:

The Open: 1. Tom **Lehman**, 2. Greg **Norman,** 3. Henry **Cotton,** 4. **Bill** Rogers, 5. **Harry** Vardon, 6. Jim **Barnes**, 7. **Tony** Jacklin, 8. J.H. **Taylor**, 9. Ian **Baker-Finch**, 10. John **Daly** or **Harold** Hilton, 11. **Gene** Sarazen, 12. **"Jock"** Hutchison

Although Jones won both Opens, he's not in the quiz.

U.S. Men's Open: 1. Johnny **Miller**, 2. Lee **Trevino**, 3. **Julius** Boros, 4. Hubert **Green**, 5. Gene **Littler**, 6. Jerry **Pate**, 7. **Hale** Irwin, 8. Andy **North**, 9. Tom **Watson**, 10. Payne **Stewart**, 11. Tommy **Armour**, 12. Johnny **Goodman**

U.S. Women's Open: 1. Se Ri **Pak**, 2. Amy **Alcott**, 3. Jan **Stephenson**, 4. **Carol** Mann, 5. **Mickey** Wright, 6. Karie **Webb**, 7. Patty **Berg**, 8. **"Babe"** Zaharias, 9. Betsy **King**, 10. Meg **Mallon**, 11. "Dottie" **Pepper**, 12. Hollis **Stacy**

Note: The most difficult answer for the Men's Open seems to be Johnny Goodman, the last amateur to win in the U.S. Men's Open, 1933. He went on to win the U.S. Amateur in 1937, joining a list of only five up to that time to win both events: Jerry Travers, Francis Ouimet, Chick Evans, and Bobby Jones. Goodman was born into a poor family, the fifth of 10 children. When his mother died, Johnny had to quit high school to go to work to help support the family, later finishing at night school. Even with all of these obstacles he was at the center of one of the greatest sports upsets in history. In 1929 at the age of 19, with his golf clubs and suitcase in hand, he grabbed a ride to San Francisco on a Union Pacific freight car. He hitchhiked to Pebble Beach for the U.S. Amateur, and in the very first round, beat Bobby Jones, the long odds-on favorite to win. Thousands of people had come to the Monterey Peninsula to watch Jones, the defending Amateur champion, capture another title as he was at the top of his game. But Goodman prevailed, one up. The offshoot of the story is that Jones then had time off so decided to visit Cypress Point, where he met Dr. Alistair MacKenzie. From that meeting Jones made the decision to invite MacKenzie to design Augusta National with him. Final note: I believe this is one of the great stories in golf and am proud to be able to share it because Johnny Goodman came from Omaha, Nebraska, my hometown.

Closing Chapter 7 is a poem from the early 1900s. It pokes a bit of fun at our concern with the scorecard. It goes like this.

If the pleasure of golf is in striking a ball
and in seven a hole you do,
I who have had fourteen in all
have had twice as much fun as you.
Sutphen Van Tassel

Observations and Quips

The psychological attraction of golf as an addictive activity is parallel to that of gambling in Las Vegas. It operates on the principle of intermittent reward. You put a quarter into a slot machine, pull the handle and you get no reward. Do it again, same result, again, again, then ka-ching, ka-ching, ka-ching, the quarters come pouring out and you experience some joy. A similar thing happens when you hit several poor shots on the golf course and then are rewarded with a few good ones…intermittent reward. That is the temptress that brings you back.

———

A Scottish county court justice was on the bench when young Robbie Black, a local caddy, was called as a witness. "Do you understand the nature of an oath?" His Honor gravely asked.

"Oh, aye, sir," answered Robbie with equal gravity. "I've carried your clubs many a time."

Golf is tough enough without extra encumbrances.

Alex Hay, brilliant teacher and author from the U.K., went on to learn a lot after he received his initial teaching tip early in his career. "While apprenticing for my PGA card as an assistant I did not receive a great deal of help on teaching from my employer. In fact about the only thing I was told was, 'You might try putting a handkerchief under their right arm. It might not help, but it won't hurt.'"

When a Canadian was asked what he meant when he described having a "Moose" on a golf hole he said, "Oh, that is five over par on a par-5." Then, putting his thumbs in his ears and wiggling his spread-apart fingers to mimic a moose, he said, "It's a 10."

QUOTES

"The old trite saying of 'one shot at a time,' it wasn't trite to me. I lived it." **Mickey Wright**

"I've spent most of my life golfing...the rest I've just wasted." **Anonymous**

"If I hit it right, it's a slice. If I hit it left, it's a hook. If I hit it straight, it's a miracle." **Anonymous**

Unpredictable Adventures on the Links

Golf is a game that offers opportunity for infinite variety. Unlike other sports where the playing field is uniform, golf is played worldwide on some 30,000 courses that are all different. Add the huge possibilities of varying weather conditions, rules situations, and the differences in the participants themselves, and you have the potential for some interesting happenings on the links.

The Man Who Cleaned Clocks

When I was a graduate student in Ann Arbor, Michigan, I found the University Blue Course to be a wonderful respite from study. Two years at the U. of M. gave me ample time to become well acquainted with that challenging layout. My game, though not what you'd describe as consistent, was on rare occasions impressive. In one instance I left the ninth green having recorded a 31 on the front side and went into the pro shop to inquire about the course record. I was told it was 63, held by Johnny Palmer, a former PGA Tour player. But I was told by the course manager, "You needn't worry about breaking it because there is a ladies outing on the back nine and it is closed for the rest of the day."

What I enjoyed most at the Blue Course was the opportunity to get up a game with some of the regulars, especially those who could "golf their ball" and were willing to put a small wager on it. There was a really nice middle-aged man who always seemed to be there when I would show up. He joined me on a lot of my rounds and certainly didn't mind playing for a few bucks, probably because he always won. It was frustrating for me. I could out-drive him by 30 yards, I was in better condition, I had better equipment, and thought I knew more about the game. But one day after he had "cleaned my clock" again he said, "Gary, sit down, I want to talk with you." So we sat together for a ginger ale and he said, "Let me tell you about playing golf. You need to learn to hit your tee shot so it simply gets into play; just so it isn't behind a tree or in some impossible lie. After that safe drive, you knock your iron up there somewhere on or around the green. Then once you are there, that's when the game really starts." Now that I think about it years later, he was one heck of a chipper and putter. But he didn't share that valuable information until the week before I left my studies at Michigan.

THE GUY HAD GUTS

"The Guy" in this case was a tall professional from Colorado. He was a Rookie of the Year on the PGA Tour, had won the Hawaiian Open, and had finished second in the U.S. Open. His name was John Schlee. John had an engaging personality, a tremendous amount of confidence, and was not shy about anything. He first appeared on tour at the time when Ben Hogan was finishing his great career. Schlee was a Hogan devotee, a disciple, although Hogan was unaware of it...until this incident.

At a tournament where both were competing, John walked into the locker room and spotted his idol putting away his golf shoes. He went up to Ben, offered his hand for a greeting, and said, "Mr. Hogan, I'm John Schlee, I want you to take care of yourself because I would like you to help me be a great player." Hogan was slightly bemused by this very friendly but forward young man, thanked him for the wish, and then left.

Later that year when the Tour came to the Dallas-Ft. Worth area, Schlee received an early phone call in his motel room. "Hold for Mr. Hogan," came the message from a secretary.

"John, this is Ben Hogan. I wanted to know if you would like to play a practice round together with me tomorrow at my club, Shady Oaks." Schlee couldn't accept quickly enough. They agreed on the time, and John hung up the phone feeling wonderful. He was going to play a private round of golf with Ben Hogan!

They met the next day at the club. After a warm-up Ben suggested they have a little game for a few bucks just to add some incentive (as if John needed it). Schlee was asked to hit first and he hooked it into the trees. Hogan then hit a perfectly positioned fade down the middle. Together they looked for John's ball and found it quickly. It was in a good lie but there were trees blocking the way to the green. Hogan suggested that John might choose to punch out into the fairway. But John, never the shrinking violet, said there was a little opening he saw between the trees. He managed to somehow drill the ball through the opening and roll it onto the green about 30 feet from the hole. Hogan hit a lovely iron to 10 feet. John got over his putt, then looked up and had this fantastic realization: "Ben Hogan is tending the flagstick for me." Schlee rolled the putt in for a birdie. Hogan missed.

On the next tee John hit first again, but this time it was pushed into a group of trees to the right. Hogan hit another drive in the center. John did not have to punch it through a small space, but he did have to curve it about 20 yards around the trees in order to hit the green. He did just that, but left a longer putt than the first one. John made it! Ben missed from eight feet. On the third hole John chipped in for another birdie and Hogan two-putted from 15 feet for par. As they walked to the fourth tee, the five-foot eight-inch Hogan looked up at the six-foot three-inch Schlee and said, "John, you are destroying everything I believe in this game."

Without missing a beat, Schlee said, "Does that mean you're not going to press?"

My Most Memorable Course

We all have memories of certain courses that made an impression on us. One that dramatically affected me early in my career is located partly in New York and partly in Connecticut; more specifically, Brewster, NY and Danbury, CT. Its uniqueness starts with the name, or names—it had two: More-Far and also Back-O-Beyond. It was built at the behest of Mr. C. V. Starr. Starr was big in the insurance industry (his company is now AIG) and had been instrumental in introducing insurance to the country of China during the 1930s.

The only members were Starr and the board of directors of the company, of which I believe there were 14. The next memorable part of this very quiet course was the golf professional. He was George Ferrier, a wonderful Scot from the old school who held the title there of "pro in perpetuity." Now that is the kind of job security some professionals might like. George, who was in his 80s, lived in Danbury and would go out to the club when there was to be some play, which wasn't every day. He would get a call from New York City saying, "George, there will be two groups on Tuesday, but no one scheduled for Wednesday, one group on Thursday." George would be at the club when the members or their guests arrived, take care of their needs, and ride around the course with them for part or all of the round. Then he'd see them off, and get ready for the next "busy" day. He was a wonderful gentleman who made your visit enjoyable no matter how your game turned out.

The most memorable highlight of this 7,000-yard gem of a course was the statuary—life-sized bronze statues on every hole. At the tee there might be a circus acrobat doing a handstand; in the bunker on a par-3, statues of two children, a boy and a girl, playing mumblety peg and jacks; later a boy flying a kite that had gotten stuck in a tree; another boy pulling a fish out of the pond that fronted one of the greens. These pieces were beautiful works of art. It was the first time I had ever thought of artistic elements enhancing the aesthetics of a golf course, but they most certainly did. This is a posthumous thank you, but George, you made that memory possible, THANKS.

A BAD DREAM

When Dr. Richard Coop and I were writing *The New Golf Mind* in the late 1970s, I was on the lookout for personal stories that had a psychological bent. This book was the first left-brain/right-brain work ever written on any sport, and we were always interested in first person anecdotal material. While I was attending "The Tournament of the Americas" in Puerto Rico as an after-dinner speaker, I found myself sitting at a large round table of guests. I inquired as to whether anyone had any stories they'd like to share about a golf experience that demonstrated the influence of the mind on the body. I immediately got a volunteer in Diana Smith, the granddaughter of the best golfer for his age in America, 80-year-old Bobby Cruickshank. Diana was a very fine player from the Pine Tree Club in Florida and was attending the tournament as a competitor. This is her story.

I was a teenage golfer in Philadelphia and the city junior champion. Because of my playing record I was accorded a spot in the U.S. Women's Open that was to be played at the Philadelphia Country Club. At the time this was way beyond my experience level. To make matters worse, I was paired in the first round with defending Women's Open Champion and certainly one of the finest women players in the world, Louise Suggs. Talk about being nervous. When I teed the ball up on the first hole of the tournament with such a large gallery surrounding everything and Ms. Suggs watching, I could feel my legs trembling. My driver swing caught only half of the ball. A low half-topped liner stopped quickly in the long grass in front of the tee. As it died you could hear the crowd utter a communal descending "Oohhh!"

Since that time I have had this recurring dream before a big tournament. I'm standing on the first tee with a huge group of people around. After I tee the ball up, I swing and miss it. Then I swing and miss it again…and then a third time. After the third attempt, Joseph Dey Jr., Executive Director of the USGA and the God figure of golf in this country, steps out of the crowd with a long wooden hook and pulls me off the tee. That has been my recurring dream.

SCENES FROM A PUBLIC COURSE

Although I have had some wonderful experiences and met some great people while employed at both private clubs and resort facilities, public golf is still the most enjoyable to me. It is the most American. All levels, all classes, show up. Yes, rich people do play public golf, right along with day laborers, housewives, the clergy, business and professional people, artists and musicians, teachers, carpenters, the retired, and the kids. It is the YM-YWCA of the sport. Interesting things happen when the mix of society arrives at the golf course together. For example:

"Scotty" was a sandy-haired weekend regular who loved his golf. He wasn't particularly good, but he was enthusiastic. Installing drywall was the work he brought to America after coming to this country from his native Scotland five years earlier. The Lane County

I love public course golf—you see some funny things.

Amateur tournament in Eugene, Oregon was coming up soon, and it was being held at our course. In trying to get a full field we encouraged all of our regular players to enter. Scotty was very reluctant. He had never played in a tournament and felt he would be too nervous. After a great deal of cajoling we secured his commitment as well as the entry fee for the Saturday/Sunday event. As we should have suspected, his inaugural attempt at tournament golf was a disaster. Shooting 15 shots over his normal game, he left the course on Saturday very depressed, feeling he needn't return. We encouraged him, almost pleaded with him, to play the next day without knowing whether or not we had been successful. His high score had earned him a 7:30 a.m. tee time on Sunday morning. For a guy who usually teed it up after work, this was a challenge. At 7:25 on Sunday Scotty had not made his appearance and it looked like the scheduled threesome for 7:30 would now be two. At that moment, pulling a wobbly cart and looking a bit wobbly himself, a disheveled Scotty appeared carrying a six-pack of Budweiser beer under his arm, looking as though his head had never hit the pillow the previous night. We rushed him toward the first tee where his fellow competitors were ready to hit their drives. All eyes in the pro shop were on Scotty as he played last in the group. Following a couple of painful-looking practice swings, he approached the ball, wound up, took a furious swing, and completely fanned everything…an air shot. The next move was classic. Without hesitation, he reached over just beyond where he had teed the ball and where he had placed the six-pack, pulled one out, popped the top, took a long swig of its contents, set it down, and promptly hit a fine drive down the middle of the fairway. It was the ultimate in "cool." Maybe it's a Scottish thing, but whatever, I don't recommend this procedure for others.

CHAMPAGNE MUSIC

There were about 160 young professionals at the five-day PGA Business School being held in Tennessee. It was the last school they had to attend and hoped to pass before they were eligible for PGA membership. This final formal learning experience was devoted largely to teaching. Classes on theory were held indoors in the morning while the practical, hands-on applications and demonstrations were outdoors in the afternoon. It was autumn, but the days were still long enough to allow for nine holes of golf after classes were finished. I paired up with three of the students, and we went out for a fast nine holes before dinner.

Reaching the par-3 fifth hole, it was "hit when you are ready," the smart way to play when you are in a hurry to finish (which we did in an hour and a half). The first player chose a 6-iron, hitting it over the green on the 160-yard hole. I was next and put it on about 20 feet from the flag. The third member of our foursome knocked it stiff…two feet away from the hole, saying to his buddy, "Let's see you get inside that." The buddy did. He knocked it into the hole for an ace with an 8-iron. He was one strong dude. Player One chipped on and two-putted for a bogey. I two-putted for my par and the guy who knocked it stiff tapped in for his birdie.

When we left the green I said, "Well, boys, we just had a Lawrence Welk hole."

"What's that?" one of the players asked.

"It's a one, and a two, and a three, and a four." My comment was delivered in precisely the manner that the king of champagne music, Mr. Lawrence Welk, would have said it when setting the tempo for a musical selection. That was his signature phrase.

A Sign for the Times

From George Lewis, PGA professional and golf book collector extraordinaire, comes this. "I worked at a course that had a par-3 hole that was about 170 yards downhill, although it played more like 150. It's funny, but on the downhill hole it seems most people tended to hit the ball right and lose it in the woods. So one of my assistants went over in the woods and put up a sign about 20 yards to the right of the green: IF YOU ARE LOOKING FOR A GOLF BALL HERE, PLEASE SEE A PGA PROFESSIONAL."

Not So Easy the First Time

She was a small one, about 95 pounds, but Jeannie was a wiry, strong, athletic woman pleased with herself because she had just successfully completed her beginning six lesson series with me. Now it was time to try it all out on the course. Just three days later, in the middle of the week and late in the afternoon, she entered the pro shop ready for her first game. Jeannie, who had just come from the hairdresser, was alone and needed to rent clubs. As I placed the clubs on the counter (an Alice Bauer starter set consisting of a 3, 5, 7, 9 putter and two woods), I apologized that I had no playing partner to accompany her on this first time out. That was okay, she said, because I had taken her out during the last lesson to show her how to get around and she felt she could do it alone. As she hoisted the bag over her shoulder we directed her to the 10th tee since the back nine, our longer par-37 side, was nearly devoid of play at that moment. She had only planned for nine holes anyway, which was fortunate as it was one of the hottest days of the year. Looking out the pro shop window I had a good view of the 10th and was pleased to see her hit a nice drive for her "first-ever official shot" on a golf course. About two hours and 30 minutes later I glanced out another window in the shop, looking this time toward the 18th green. There was a small hill that needed to be negotiated after leaving the green in order to get back to the clubhouse. Jeannie had reached the top of the hill looking as though she had just crossed the Sahara desert. Perspiring profusely, with sweat stains evident on her clothing, the hair so neatly coiffed at the start now dangling in several directions, and the bag no longer on her shoulder but instead cradled in front of her with both arms wrapped around it. In that condition she staggered into the shop. Jeannie dropped the bag on the counter, looked up at me, and in an exhausted voice said, *"I'd rather have a baby."* Actually, she did have a couple of babies after that and played 18 holes regularly. But Jeannie will never forget that original nine.

Caddies Say the Darndest Things

My friend from church, Bob Marker, is a retired CEO of one of the largest advertising companies in America. He loves his golf and once played to a four handicap. With an office in New York, a good share of his golf was played in Westchester County. It was late April, early in the northern season, and he was engaged in a game as a guest at the Westchester C.C. While this was business golf, there still was a wager on the outcome. Bob was not having a particularly good day, scoring higher than would be expected of someone with his talent. On the 16th hole Bob overheard the caddies arguing. It sounded like they were fighting about money. Suspecting that they were wagering on the match, Marker went over to his caddy and said, "Are you betting on the game?"

"Yes, sir, we are."

"Are you betting on me?" was the next question and again the same response.

"Yes, sir."

Then Marker continued, "Why are you betting on me?"

"Well, Mr. Marker, I watched you on the practice tee, you've got a good swing and I said to myself, we got us a horse here today. This man got some game. Then I looked at your right hand, it's tan, you've been in Florida all winter, you're ready to go. Then I saw your bag tag. It says Winged Foot is where you play and they don't have phony handicaps at that place. But frankly, Mr. Marker," the caddy said, looking his man right in the eye, *"You've been a big disappointment!"*

Marker claims it is the funniest thing anyone has ever said to him on a golf course.

It Is a Game of Timing

Four young guys were playing their regular weekend game and had a few bets on the line. They arrived at a par-4 hole that bordered a busy street on the left, separated from the course only by a sidewalk and a four-strand barbed wire fence. The first three players hit a variety of drives down the fairway, nothing unusual. But the fourth player in the group did not follow suit. His drive was a wild hook that shot through the fence, over the sidewalk, and hit the back tire of a passing bus. The ball rebounded wildly back toward the course, miraculously ending up in the fairway in good position. The three players watching were incredulous! Then they broke up when their pal turned to them and promptly let them know the reason for his good fortune. *"You've got to know the bus schedule,"* was his smiling explanation.

I Know How to Read the Greens

At a modest Midwestern country club they were hosting a charity pro-am that had attracted a few PGA Tour players. One of them was former Masters Champion George Archer. Archer was known as one of the Tour's best putters. He had grown up at Harding Park in San Francisco where he used to spend hours putting for money. George was paired in the pro-am with an old doctor who had been a member of the club for 40 years. The doctor was more than just a bit on the crotchety side as well as being tight with his pennies. He even had to be talked into coming up with the money to get into the event in the first place.

Archer's team with the doctor aboard was doing well. It looked as though they had a chance to win the team event. That meant a little more of a payday for Archer, so when the doctor knocked his ball onto the par-3 17th George thought he would add his years of experience to the reading of the doctor's 20-foot putt. He

George Archer's advice wasn't needed.

got behind the doctor's line and said, "This one is going to break about six inches left, so play it three balls out to the right."

The doctor jumped right in and said, "No it doesn't, that's a straight putt." George disagreed but the doctor was adamant. "Look," he said, "I've been a member here nearly all of my life, and that's a straight putt."

"Okay," said George as he backed off.

Doc hit the putt and it came roaring across the green. It was traveling straight at the hole but obviously way too hard. It hit the back of the hole and jumped about a foot up in the air, dropping back down into the cup! It looked impossible but it went in. "See," Doc said, "I told you it was a straight putt."

Archer looked at him and responded, "When you hit them that hard, Doc, they are all straight."

Running at Pebble Beach

When Japanese golfers started coming to the United States in greater numbers during the 1970s, they got the label of being "slow players." This may have been the case initially because getting on a golf course in Japan was an infrequent event due to the cost. Many players who came here just didn't have enough experience in getting around the course while facing situations that were never presented to them at the driving ranges where they learned their golf swings. The Japanese, however, are very conscientious about manners. Therefore, as the word got to them about being slow, they would often run between shots on the course.

A golf professional from the New England PGA had never visited the west coast of the United States. During one winter season a few years ago he decided to take in that coast all the way from the state of Washington to Southern California. One of his most anticipated stops was going to be at Pebble Beach. It was a chilly afternoon in January when he got there, having called the head professional in advance to make arrangements to play. The wind was up and the golf course activity was quiet. When he checked in, the head pro apologized for not having someone for him to play with, but said, "The course is really open. The last players to go out were two Japanese guys about 40 minutes ago. Take your umbrella and rain suit just in case and just go out and enjoy yourself."

Our New England pro was doing just that when he caught up to the two players in front of him on the par-5 sixth hole. They were in the fairway approaching the green when one of them hit and ran (not unusual) up near the green, *then ran back*. His partner hit next, and they both ran ahead. He watched them finish number six. Then he played his shot up to the green, and while getting ready to putt looked over at the twosome. They were now on the magnificent 110-yard par-3, which rested on the precipice above the ocean. As he anticipated playing this famous hole, what caught his attention was that the first player on the tee hit his ball, ran forward, then ran back, just as he had done on the previous hole. After the second player hit, they both ran to the green again. When the pro arrived on the seventh tee, the two Japanese players stood aside on the green and politely waved him to play ahead. He hit a great knockdown 8-iron into the stiff breeze and made it to the front of the skinny green. After being invited to hole out he did so. But before leaving for the grand eighth hole with its daring shot across the chasm, he said, "Excuse me, but I was wondering why are you guys running to the ball and then running back?"

"Oh, the golf course is most difficult," one replied. "Many bad shots. Only one ball left...we must share!"

Just a Bit of Understanding

Jack Lupton is one of the captains of industry. As the largest Coca-Cola bottler in the United States, he follows his grandfather who had been one of the first. If you visit Chattanooga, Tennessee, you will see the evidence of Lupton charitable giving all over the city, particularly in the Riverpark. One of Jack Lupton's favorite projects, though, was the development of the Honors Club, "the Augusta National of Tennessee," and that is meant in the most complimentary way. But even "captains" get their occasional comeuppance, as is reflected in this story.

Lupton was a guest playing with friends at a private southern club. He had been assigned a caddy who not only had a strong regional accent and a slight speech defect, but also mumbled when he spoke. The group had played the front nine with Lupton frequently mentioning that half the time he couldn't understand what his caddy was saying. It was irritating him. On the back side they reached the first par-3, which was 155 yards over water. Lupton asked his caddy what he thought he should hit.

"A syss iron," mumbled the caddy.

"What?" said Lupton. "Speak up, man. I can't understand a thing you are saying. Speak up!"

The caddy handed his player a 6-iron, which Lupton hit fat into the water. Then the caddy took a step toward Lupton looking him dead in the eye and said, "You wet. You understand that?" And this time he didn't mumble.

Who Said Golf Was Hard?

Jimmy Nichols was a one-armed golf professional who toured the country giving playing exhibitions. Performing before a good-sized crowd at an old-style New England course, he teed off on the first hole, a 320-yard sharp dogleg par-4 with a level fairway that then turned left and dropped off sharply some 20 feet to the small green below. Because of the surrounding trees you would normally hit a long iron out near the top of the hill and then a wedge to the green. But Nichols, using his one arm, hit a sharply hooking drive around the corner. The ball rolled down the hill and into the cup for an ace. The crowd went wild, but Jimmy threw down his club as in disgust and made one of the best impromptu quips I have ever heard, "I quit. This course is too easy."

Moving Up in the World

One of the best executives in the golf-manufacturing world is Rick Papreck, now with Cobra. During the many years that he served the Tommy Armour Company as the national sales manager he worked hard at motivating people to be their best. One of the PGA Tour players, Jim Gallagher Jr., who was on the Armour staff, got a taste of Rick's efforts to motivate when Rick offered to caddy for Jim if Gallagher qualified for The PGA Championship. It must have worked because Gallagher started to play better and made the field. One thing working in Papreck's favor was that The PGA was being played at Kemper Lakes in Chicago, which was where the Armour Company was headquartered. The week of the tournament arrived and Papreck, the golf executive, changed from a white shirt and tie to a caddy bib for a week. While he was in pretty good shape for an executive, he was not quite ready to carry a tour bag in the Chicago August heat. But he did it, and got stronger after each practice round.

It was Thursday, and now things counted. Gallagher played well enough and Papreck caddied well enough, but what ensued was worth the day's effort. It had to do with the scorer. During the round Rick couldn't help but feel he knew the woman that was working their group, yet he couldn't quite place her...until the 18th hole. Then it hit him. She was the daughter of a wealthy man who belonged to Indian Hill, an exclusive Chicago suburb course. They used to play together, father and daughter, and Papreck used to caddy for them when he was a kid.

When the last hole was completed, the scorecards exchanged, and equipment set aside, Rick went over to the lady and said, "You don't remember me, do you?" She replied that he looked familiar but she didn't know why. Then Rick told her. "You used to play golf with your father at Indian Hill, and I used to caddy for you."

She smiled, paused, and looking at his caddy outfit said, "My, you've done very well for yourself, haven't you?"

I REALLY FELT SORRY...FOR AWHILE

One of the better players to come out of the Wisconsin professional ranks has been Steve Bull. He spent some years on the PGA Tour before heading to Tripoli C.C. to serve as the head professional for 38 years. Steve was a real competitor in any club pro event at all levels, but in his middle years he developed a terrible case of the yips. I am not talking about a simple flinch, I am referring to a "spastic" stroke that caused him to actually jump in the air. Really!...both feet would leave the ground. But the interesting thing about it and the disconcerting part for his opponents was that he learned to consistently make those nervous short putts that way…he would go airborne and the putt would go in.

I was playing behind Steve's group in an event at the PGA facility in Port St. Lucie. My round was going very well for scoring but I was irritated by my lack of focus on several holes that let a better score get away. After a strong drive on the 18th hole I was standing in the fairway only a wedge distance from the green and talking to myself. "C'mon, Gary, your mind has been all over the place. Focus, for God's sake!" I could see Steve putting on the 18th green. There was the little jump but apparently he missed, because I could see him having to tap in. I felt for him.

The focus talk I gave to myself must have worked because I hit the flagstick from about 95 yards out and made the putt for a 69. Feeling pretty good about my round and myself, I turned in my card and went into the clubhouse where I saw Steve. Ready to tell him about my score and hear about his woes I asked "How did you do today, Steve?"

"Sixty-four," was his answer.

I walked away not feeling too sorry anymore for my jumping friend and certainly not ready to brag about my round.

SOME PRESSURE IS JUST TOO MUCH

The person who had this experience some 20 years earlier told this story to me.

> I was 18 years old and a junior member at a good golf club in the Philadelphia district. There was an annual mixed team tournament in the area, and since I was one of the best players at our club, a fellow member asked me to be her partner. She was a very attractive

blond divorcee in her early 40s who played a solid game. I felt the two of us might do well together in this tournament.

On the final day of the event we were near the lead as we came to one of the closing holes, a short par-3 that had lots of trouble surrounding the green. My partner and I were standing together as the group in front of us played. She turned to me and quietly said, "Get this one close and I will go to bed with you tonight."

Picture the next scene. Me, an 18-year-old virgin, standing on the tee, my mind racing about what had just been said, trying to get the right pictures in my mind and focusing on why I was on the tee in the first place. It didn't work…I shanked it out-of-bounds. She missed the green, and we lost the event. While walking to the green I remember her saying to me, "I thought you were good under pressure."

My response was, *"Not that kind of pressure."*

MUSIC TO SOOTHE THE SAVAGE STROKE

Earlier in the book I mentioned Kent Country Club and will never forget playing there with Dr. Swanson. I had made a Michigan trip to nearby Ferris State University in Big Rapids. It is the home of the first Professional Golf Management Program in the country. Dr. Lowell LeClair, a former golf professional and a good player, was the program's director. After our work was finished he suggested that we go to Grand Rapids for a golf game at Kent. He had lined up a very attractive match with Dick Ford (brother to President Jerry Ford) and Dr. Al Swanson (president of the Hand Surgeons Association of the World).

When we arrived I was impressed by the friendliness of Ford, much like his famous brother, and the athletic look of Dr. Swanson. The doctor's attire of walking shorts and golf shirt revealed a body that could play fullback in the Big Ten. It didn't take long in the round to discover that Dr. Swanson was plenty long off the tee. He hit the first green in regulation, and then it started. I have seen bad cases of the yips before, particularly when the player gets close to the hole, but even putting cross-handed, the doc had 'em and he wasn't selective. He yipped from both long and short. It was painful to watch, yet more painful, I'm sure, to experience. After nine holes it appeared to me that the only guaranteed way Doc was going to get many pars or birdies was with some generous "gimme" putts.

I don't know if it was coincidence or not, but in my bag I carried a Walkman cassette player and headset. The previous month I had been working on the effect of a specific kind of music on relaxation. Aware that alpha rhythm brain waves are desirable for a calm but alert performance in activities, I had a music studio create seven original compositions on a synthesizer, all in alpha rhythm. On the 10th tee, after our drives, I asked Dr. Swanson to try something. "Put on this headset and listen to the music while walking the hole rather than riding in the cart." He did. Walking to his long tee shot in the right rough he proceeded to hit another good short iron onto the green. The first putting stroke with the Walkman on wasn't pure, but it was better. He got down in two putts for a par. On the next hole the stroke was even smoother. By the time we reached the 12th green, a par-3 that the doctor had hit from the tee, the now "walking/listening physician" made the prettiest stroke you can imagine, lipping out and calmly cleaning up the tap-in. Dick Ford looked at me and said, *"I'll be damned! He's been my partner for the last five member/guests, and I have never seen him make a stroke like that."* It was music calming the "Savage Stroke."

I used the same technique in playing my first-ever major, the U.S. Senior Open at Pinehurst. With my headset on and my alpha music playing, I stood between Jack Nicklaus and Gary Player on the practice tee and felt as calm as if I were lying on the beach, listening to the ocean surf.

HAD TO HEAT 'EM UP

The national meeting of the PGA of America was being held in Seattle during December. Maybe the room rates were good, but the weather certainly wasn't, at least not for those of us coming from Florida. The day before the meeting was to start I got an opportunity to play Sahalee Country Club, which several years later became a site for The PGA Championship. When we started our round the temperature was right around 34 degrees with a fine misty rain in the air. With no wind and the right clothing it wasn't that uncomfortable. The first time I noticed something unusual was on the back nine. Facing a four-foot putt I hit it with what would normally have been the correct force but the ball came up dramatically short. At first I was baffled. Then I looked closely at my putter and saw that a thin coating of ice covered it and that had deadened the force. Apparently the temperature had dropped a couple more degrees from when we started and now was at freezing or below. The cold metal combined with the moisture in the air was causing not only my putter, but also all of my iron clubs, to "ice up." To finish the round I had to first put my hand around the club head to melt the ice before hitting the shot. I would bet that not many golfers have ever heard about, let alone had, that experience.

GET OFFA' THERE!

One of the strangest sights I ever witnessed on a golf course was at the Tualatin Country Club just south of Portland, Oregon. A feature of the short but tight course was the towering Douglas firs that lined the fairways and made you think twice about using your driver. This was particularly true on the ninth hole. There you teed off in the valley, some 30 feet below the fairway that rose abruptly 175 yards ahead of you to a plateau, and then continued on toward the green. The hole was short, maybe 305 yards, and could be driven with a long and accurate shot. But the play of choice was a fairway wood or long iron to the top of the hill in order to keep out of the woods.

After my group had finished the hole there was a delay. I happened to look over toward the foursome on the ninth green. One of the members of the group was just pulling out the flagstick to let another player tap in his two-footer after a good chip. The player who was putting made a casual "taking it for granted" stroke and when he did, the ball actually stuck to his putter face! You would have died laughing to see the reaction. He launched into a spasmodic dance and wiggle of his arms to get the ball off the clubface and into the hole. His efforts caused the ball to disengage itself from the club and drop nearby. He then tapped it in for some kind of score that the rules official was going to have to determine.

But what was the cause of the ball sticking in the first place? He had tried to drive the green but had pushed the shot into the woods where the ball solidly hit a tree. Apparently it struck a spot where resin was leaking from the tree. Not noticing anything on the ball, he had pitched it out to a spot in front of the green. From there he made a good chip to where his adventure for what he thought was going to be an easy par took place. The ball had apparently rolled to a position where the resin on the ball matched up to the face of the putter, and that's what ruined his putt. While it didn't go in, it did produce the best laugh of the day. The final ruling: He played it from where it dropped and made bogey.

SHORT COURSE

A new club member from India had just finished a series of beginner lessons and showed up at the course to play on a Saturday afternoon. It was his first time to actually play, with the exception of the one hole that he completed with the professional when his lessons had ended. The pro had taken him out on number one, showed him the purpose of the tee markers, had him hit some shots from the fairway, finished putting on the first green, then as they rode back in, explained some basic rules to the novice. On that Saturday afternoon the course wasn't heavily booked, but the professional did notice some congestion at the first tee and wondered what was going on. His course ranger appeared at about that time from the back nine and got on the walkie-talkie to explain. "We have this new player out here who has played the first hole three times and then comes back and starts again. Does he know there are more holes he can play or does he plan to play this one 18 times?" Apparently, he didn't know, and was just going to keep playing number one.

I Guess It Was the Look

Being on the Golf Digest Professional Panel with Paul Runyan, Sam Snead, Bob Toski, Cary Middlecoff, Davis Love Sr., John Jacobs, Jim Flick, and Eddie Merrins was more than a treat, it was an education. That lineup includes four people in the Golf Teacher's Hall of Fame and two others in the World Golf Hall of Fame. As interesting as the conversation was about the topics that the editors challenged us with, even more so was the opportunity to play golf with these people during the round that accompanied all panel meetings. But to my regret, of all the times we did this, I never was paired with Snead.

Sam played at Pine Tree Golf Club, in Boynton Beach, Florida, during the winter. My good friend Bob Ross, the head professional, called me one time and said, "How would you like to get a game with Sam?"

My reply was an enthusiastic, "You bet I would."

"Well, he's going to want to play for something," Bob continued.

"That's fine, it will be worth it," I replied and the game was set.

In my golf library is a book that Sam did with Al Stump entitled *The Education of a Golfer,* and in it Sam revealed the observations he made while watching competitors in the heat of battle. When a medal play tournament got down to the winner being decided between just a couple of players, Sam said it became like match play. At that point he would look for any signs of nervousness in his opponent. He told of one player who used to start scratching his butt when he was nervous; another who started lighting up cigarettes one after the other; and one who used to get a white streak down his face when the going got tough. "That's when I knew I had 'em," said Sam.

Since Sam was "going to want to play for something," I was

thinking on the drive down to Pine Tree what my strategy was going to be to avoid a large financial loss. I finally came up with one. When I saw Sam, I would go up to him and say, "Sam, how would you like to make this game interesting?" I could just see the smile coming on his face and the sparkle in his eye...until I continued. "Since you've won 82 official tournaments on the PGA Tour and I haven't won any, you give me two shots a side

Sam was putting side-saddle.

and then it might be interesting." Great plan but it didn't work.

When I arrived Sam was on the putting green. He immediately came over to me and said, "Gary, you and me be partners."

So we rode together and played the front side. After I got over my jitters I started to notice, *I'm driving the ball past Snead. I'm hitting it inside of him on several holes and he is doing that side-saddle putting thing. We're playing even.* Actually, we weren't because he shot 36 and I shot 37, but nonetheless my bravado increased and on the way to the backside I looked over and said, "I'll play you for 10 on the back nine."

He looked at me kind of funny, and I hoped he understood that 10 was just $10 and didn't have some hidden meaning like for 100 or 1,000.

The 10th hole is a dogleg left par-5 that is reachable in two, but you have to position your drive just right to do it. I did, and hit the green with a 4-iron, sinking the putt for eagle. Snead looked at me and said, "You're getting awful good awful fast." He birdied the tough 11th par-3 to go even and that is the way we stayed up to number 16. The problem is, I had hit it to six feet on both number 14 and number 15 and left both putts short. Not a good sign…I was choking.

Sixteen is a 666-yard par-5 and my score was birdie four; one up with two to go. I was first on the tee at number 17 and thinking, *I'm going to be able to tell my grandchildren that the first time I ever played Sam Snead in a match I beat him.* It was a bit premature. Sam's feet were in my sight straight across from where I was teeing up the ball. For what reason I will never know, but I glanced up to see his face. Sam had his arms folded; his straw hat pulled down, and was staring at me like a tight-lipped beady-eyed killer. The thought immediately ran through my mind…*My God, I wonder if I have a white streak running down my face.* THAT DID IT! I push-skied my drive, made a bogie…bogeyed number 18 and lost by one. I guess it was the look.

OBSERVATIONS AND QUIPS

A caddy who was looping for a Mr. and Mrs. Jones suffered through the first two holes as they were hitting all grounders and scoring 10s and 11s. After the second hole he made this astute observation, "I'm sorry," he said, "but this is golf, not bowling."

———————

When the Kiawah Island Golf Course (which hosted the Ryder Cup) was first opened, the assessment of the links was that it had the toughest finishing 18 holes in golf.

———————

Homero Blancas, the "boy wonder," who once shot a 55 in a tournament while an amateur, was able to win an event during his second year on the PGA Tour. Later in his pro career, after a bad putting round, he figured out his problem. "I was reading them in Spanish and putting them in English."

———————

Here are some caddy comments that leave you scratching your head:

A player asking his caddy how a putt looked was told, "Slightly straight."

When one caddy was asked how far it was to the green he said, "Halfway."

Another was asked by his player (Dutch Harrison) if he could get home from here, "Geez Mr. Dutch, I don't even know where you live."

Finally, in a group of four ladies on the ninth green with four caddies, one of the women asked the rookie caddy "Who's away?"

He looked around quickly and said, "Nobody, ma'am, everybody is here that we started with."

Quotes

"We went tweet, tweet, tweet, tweet, par, tweet, tweet, par, tweet and that adds up to a 29!" PGA Tour player **Willie Wood's caddy**

"The man who thinks he can teach himself golf by practicing his own ideas on two afternoons a week is paying a very poor compliment to a very great game." **Harry Vardon**

"I never wanted to be a millionaire, I just wanted to live like one." **Walter Hagen**

What's Important?

It seemed like it just was going to be another corporate outing, meet a few guys from a company I may or may not have ever heard of, play a round of golf with them, give a few tips, tell some stories, ask about their jobs and families, have a lemonade or whatever afterward, and say goodbye. Sometimes you exchange business cards and occasionally stay in contact with them afterward, but mostly it becomes only a memory preserved with a picture taken on the first tee that now resides in a remote drawer at your house. This outing at PGA National in Palm Beach Gardens was different. Not the venue, as I had been there as either a member or teacher since it opened, and not the format because it was the same old best ball of the group with handicap. What was different was my cart-riding partner. Now, most of the people you meet playing golf are pleasant. It's that kind of game. Then there are some who are special. My playing companion sitting next to me that day was one of those "special" people. He was in his mid-sixties, from Kansas City and the owner of a wholesale appliance company. His golf handicap was an unimpressive 18, and that's about the way he played. But it wasn't his golf that caught my attention; it was his demeanor. Quiet, yet interesting, polite but with strength of conviction, conversant about many things other than himself, a family man and obviously one of good character. It turned out to be one of those male bonding situations, where you know right away that you like each other and that you were going to have a good time together.

After the round was over, the scores were posted without our team being in the winning column. Our other two partners left after one drink. Then as the two of us sat together my new friend said to me, "Gary, I really had a most enjoyable time with you on the course today. Thank you for the companionship and for the swing tips that I'm sure will be useful. I learned a lot from you, but now I would like to teach you something in exchange."

"Certainly," I said, "I'd love to hear what you have to share."

"Golf," he said, "didn't appear in my life until I was 52 years old. But when it did I was hooked. I loved the game. Couldn't seem to get enough. After starting at a local municipal course, getting lessons, and trying to reach that first milestone of breaking 100 I decided to join a private club. Wolf Creek was my choice, just outside of town, a course with a strong reputation and a good professional, Jeff Burrey. At Wolf Creek my game started to improve. I became a regular, shooting scores in the low 90s, occasionally visiting the high 80s. During that first year at the club I found three other guys who were as bad as I was. We made a foursome every Saturday, with a one o'clock start. It was a bright spot in my life that I looked forward to every week. In fact, on a summer Saturday if I had a big customer in my showroom and they were contemplating ordering $250,000 in appliances but it was getting close to noon, I would turn them over to an associate, saying, 'I'm sorry, but I have an important engagement to attend.' Once on the course my group would make a few bets, needle one another, laugh at each other's bad shots, tell stories, have a shower with the kidding continuing, end with a drink, and head home. Surprisingly we didn't socialize outside the golf gathering, but our weekly times together were special. That is how it went for several years.

"During this past winter one of my group died suddenly of a heart attack. Another had a severe stroke and won't be able to play golf again. The third moved to Phoenix. When I went back to Wolf Creek this spring it wasn't the same. Oh, it was the same course; my equipment was the same; the game itself was the same; but it wasn't the same. That is when I realized it is not just the game. *It is the people you meet and the friendships that you develop in golf that are really important.* Gary, don't you ever forget it."…and he left. That's what's important.

Competitors and friends Lonnie Nielsen and Bob Ford.

Postscript

Yes, golf has been, and continues to be for me, a "ball." So my dear reader, I wish for you what some wise person once penned as their desire:

1. To be where I want to be

2. Do what I want to do

3. Be with someone I want to be with

4. And do something as well as I can.

I have tried to make these four come true in my own life, and hope that has been demonstrated in this book.